Praise for *We Heard the Heavens Then*

"Minu-Sepehr recalls a defining moment in his country's history, a moment that sums up the tension between secular and religious, West and East until today. The politically astute should investigate."

—*Library Journal*

"The strength of *We Heard the Heavens Then* is Minu-Sepehr's keen eye and wealth of detail. He captures the exuberance, naiveté and anxiety of childhood, as well as a son's hero worship of his father."

—*The Oregonian*

"Written with the honesty and humor representative of childhood mixed with the longing and acceptance of an adult separated from his homeland, this memoir offers an insider's perspective on a country . . . that often remains a mystery to Western people."

—*Publishers Weekly* (a *Publishers Weekly*
"Top Ten Memoir" for Spring 2012)

"Aria Minu-Sepehr's memoir about growing up in Iran before the fall of the Shah is an exquisitely told tale brimming with sensuality, humor, and humanity. Minu-Sepehr vividly captures the intense yearning and bewilderment of childhood as he, like a modern-day Shahrazad, unravels a rich and unforgettable tapestry of true-life stories set in a country on the verge of revolution. *We Heard the Heavens Then* is a son's eloquent tribute to his father and to the beloved country he had to leave behind."

—Mira Bartók, author of *New York Times* bestselling
The Memory Palace

"*We Heard the Heavens Then* is an extraordinary story of a child who sees his Paradise turn into Hell, an exhilarating work that reveals the delusions of the Shah's regime about modernity and exposes the terrifying nature of the turbaned beards' dogma. An intelligent, witty, honest, and hilariously funny, but also heartbreaking memoir. A remarkable book written by a brilliant writer. A great read."

—Fadhil al-Azzawi, author of *The Last of the Angels*

"There are photographs that define a nation in a particular time. In his down-to-earth childhood memoir of Iran just before, during, and after the revolution, Minu-Sepehr catches precisely the pulse of a country as it appears to hurl itself headlong into the abyss. And, especially, in the sympathetic portrayal of the author's father, an Air Force General and jet fighter ace, we get a soaring view of what every Iranian has often imagined—of what might have been and wasn't."

—Salar Abdoh, author of *The Poet Game* and *Opium*

"*We Heard the Heavens Then* grasps the reader from page one; it is a brilliantly written memoir of a time most have forgotten. The book has a sensual, humorous, spirited, and compassionate voice throughout, while telling a remarkable story."

—New and Good Reading

"A compelling book."

—Broken Teepee

"This book is a fascinating story of family and politics, a story of what is possible and how fast it can all go away if not nurtured constantly."

—Book Him Danno

"At its core, [*We Heard the Heavens Then*] is really a human story about how a family finds that the country where they have lived for just about forever can no longer be a safe home."

—A Bookish Affair

"A truly emotional tale that takes you in from the beginning to the end."

—Dad of Divas

We Heard the Heavens Then

A Memoir of Iran

ARIA MINU-SEPEHR

☙

SIMON & SCHUSTER PAPERBACKS

New York   London   Toronto   Sydney   New Delhi

SIMON & SCHUSTER PAPERBACKS
A Division of Simon & Schuster, Inc.
1230 Avenue of the Americas
New York, NY 10020

First Simon & Schuster trade paperback edition April 2013

SIMON & SCHUSTER PAPERBACKS and colophon are trademarks of Simon & Schuster, Inc.

Photographs on pages xii and 237 are courtesy of the author.

For information about special discounts for bulk purchases,
please contact Simon & Schuster Special Sales at 1-866-506-1949
or business@simonandschuster.com.

The Simon & Schuster Speakers Bureau can bring authors to your live event.
For more information or to book an event contact the Simon & Schuster Speakers Bureau
at 1-866-248-3049 or visit our website at www.simonspeakers.com.

Manufactured in the United States of America

1   3   5   7   9   10   8   6   4   2

The Library of Congress has catalogued the hardcover edition as follows:

Minu-Sepehr, Aria.
We heard the heavens then : a memoir of Iran / Minu-Sepehr.
p. cm.
1. Minu-Sepehr, Aria. 2. Iranians—20th century—Biography. 3. Iran—History—Revolution,
1979. 4 Iran—Politics and government—20th century. I. Title.
955.05'3092
[B]
2011279869

ISBN 978-1-4516-5218-5
ISBN 978-1-4516-5219-2 (pbk)
ISBN 978-1-4516-5221-5 (ebook)

for my father,
who showed me boundless love

❦

and for the men and women who were killed
because they believed in progress

Contents

We Heard the Heavens Then

☙

Prologue

February 15, 1979

Pictures of the first four men who were killed covered the front page of the newspaper. Men I knew, scattered in puddles of black blood. The pencil-thin, demure Naji had been a regular at our house. Aunt Z used to tell dirty jokes that made him blush, made him melt into our big couch. After a year of strikes, sneers, and street fights, the revolutionary movement had officially seized power, and the execution was its first statement. It wouldn't be its last. One by one, my father's military colleagues began to fall. Familiar faces in black-and-white. Caved-in cheeks.

The day our air force ace, Nader, appeared in the paper, my mother screamed. She clenched the paper and fell onto the couch. Legend said Iran's skies belonged to two men, Nader and my father—rivals in speed, altitude, daredevil aerobatics, and aerial marksmanship. Nightfall. Bubbi, my nanny, shuffled in from the kitchen with a tray of tea, as if to say, I'm not sure what else to bring. Tradition had given us a ritual for any human experience—watermelon for the longest night of the year, a bowl of water spilled behind a traveler for a safe return, seeds of rue burnt to keep evil spirits away, jasmine for lovers—but Nader's death exhausted the imagination. The adults reached for the dainty tea glasses only to watch the steam weave impenetrable messages in the air above.

Prologue

I was ten years old: My greatest fear up until that point was the end of fifth grade. There were horror stories about the terminal exam, and if I survived it, there was the terrifying prospect of middle school and giant eighth graders. All of that seemed to fade away with a thousand new questions. Why were our family friends being slaughtered? What had they done? On whose order were they being murdered? Weren't we in charge of the armed forces? Didn't we make the government? Why was America being blamed? Was it wrong to like skateboards and faded jeans and Cookie Monster? Looking at my family, I only saw blank faces confronting a thousand questions of their own. Eerie quiet. Aloof stares. Sudden, seemingly unprovoked quivers and weeping. Yet with each passing day, each report of another rooftop execution, I came closer to asking, What of you, Father? When will they come for you?

1

"Corrupter of the Land"

For as long as I could remember, my father had been a general. Growing up in the air force, around armed forces, I had become adept at recognizing ranks. One look at someone's uniform, at their silver stripes, bronze asters, or gold stars, and I could tell exactly where they stood, who obeyed whom. In the last four years, Baba wore two stars and an imperial crown on his epaulettes; he was a major general, commander of a sensitive base in Isfahan. All eyes were on the operation: The king considered it a glowing achievement to bring the most sophisticated fighter jet in the world to Iran. On the American side, handing over a national secret to a country bordering the Soviet Union was risky. Could Baba establish order? At the height of the cold war, would one of our pilots be lured by communist propaganda, defect, and give away an American technological advantage? Every move, even my grade-school life, had to be scrutinized.

The barren setting of the base, on the high plateau of a forbidding desert, was unlike the city it bordered. Isfahan, the city, was fed by a river, nurtured for centuries, tree-stippled and verdant. In contrast, our air force base was a wasteland situated at the foot of towering, azure mountains. If one traveled in the direction of the mountains, the desert terrain quickly turned rocky, pocked, and undulating. The strewn fragments of basalt and obsidian were signs that in this land monumental calm periodically gave way to sudden, convulsive upheavals.

The infertile landscape of our home had a formative influence on me. My desert: a vast carpet of undifferentiated barrenness stretching away in serene quietude. My mountains: impassive overseers of my youth. Against this backdrop the sun revealed its various faces like clockwork—starlike at dawn, canary yellow by midmorning, a diffuse blaze in the afternoon. One glance at the sky and I could tell when school would end, when the guards outside our driveway would change shifts, when my father would arrive, or when supper would appear on the table.

A month before everything changed, Baba moved to Tehran, the capital city, to assume a new post with a new star. My mother, my caretaker, and I were to follow during the New Year's break. Along with school, the entire nation would shut down in March, on the first day of spring. A weeklong celebration would ensue—presents, picnics, Grandmother's house a revolving door of guests. But that year, in the dust of the revolution, spring's tender blossoms came and went without notice.

On the day the regime fell, we left the base in a hurry and with hearts pounding. My mother packed two satchels, swept up our poodle, and told Bubbi to leave whatever she was doing and get in the car.

"Your dad's already with Mamman Ghodsi and your brother is safe in America. The rest can go to hell," she explained to me.

"What's going to happen to my toys?" I asked.

"Room, house, this goddamn air force base . . . it can all go up in flames. What precious years I sacrificed. From ruin to ruin. And this is my thank-you."

"But Missus, I left stew bubblin' on the stove," said Bubbi, puzzled.

"They'll come looking for the baby only to find a peed-in bed." My mother was engaged in some heated mental dialogue, just not with us.

Arriving in Tehran the way we did was disorienting; the revolutionary fervor was at its peak. But even in good times, the capital was a disaster compared to the base: tortuous streets, reckless drivers, ceaseless neon lights. Islamic architecture stood next to glass-clad buildings or European neoclassic designs, an occasional Chinese pagoda appearing out of nowhere. Billboards advertised Indian Darjeeling tea, William Friedkin's *The Exorcist*, "as white as snow with Snow laundry detergent," and Sakura Mikado—the latest craze in Japanese wristwatches.

Overlaid on this visual jangle, political graffiti turned every blank wall into a revolutionary message board. The plastered-on slogans were austere, even didactic. "The triumph of the worker!" a Marxist slogan celebrated. "One person, one vote," preached the National Front. "The anus," declared an inscription in neat calligraphy, "should never be wiped with the right hand. [Signed] Imam Khomeini." There was a private dialogue in these messages, a war of wits, and a particular faction's street cred could be assessed by the permanence of its markings. The mujahideen might start the week strong. By Wednesday, the Marxists would have the upper hand. But by week's end, all would be smeared by the Party of God—"War / the only way to liberty / Faith, jihad, martyrdom / the only way to prosperity."

Entering a new school two-thirds of the way through fifth grade was a worry that paled in comparison to the threat of my father's execution. And as though Baba anticipated the inevitable, he went out of his way to spend each afternoon with me, running pointless errands before dinner.

"Where are we going?" I wanted to know.

"Oh, to see how things are coming along."

"What things?"

"It's interesting that we immediately put value on the *things* and not on the act of seeing. The verb, I'm thinking, is more worthy of our attention. How do you see? What things do you choose to see? Whom do you see it with?" he mused.

This was the revolution's lasting result—you could ask the simplest question and receive a cryptic, off-the-wall answer.

We arrived at an excavated site, a hole big enough to swallow a house.

"Future site of a building. Aren't you glad you came?" my father said.

"What building?"

"A house. Technically yours and your brother's. Consider me your contractor." My parents' dream house. Their luck in buying property in a neighborhood before it became chic. So *this,* a hole in the ground, was what my mother billed as our new home overlooking the city? Stacks of architectural plans, the nightly fussing over the placement of windows, doors, and closets. Weekends comparing different styles of banisters and newel posts forming a *Gone with the Wind* staircase. The groundbreaking. The recent quagmire of unsettled legal issues, as anyone with "official" capacity had abdicated his position.

"What do we do now?" I asked. How was anything possible in the chaos of the revolution?

"Good question. We go and drag the little mice out of their hiding holes and send them back to work. Or find someone bold enough to say, By the power vested in me . . ."

We got back in the car and headed into Tehran's perpetual rush hour. Standstill traffic made me restive. The blare of a revolutionary song on someone's radio shivered my spine. I couldn't tell if I was terrified or excited by martial rhythms, the catchy tunes about resistance, brotherhood, and martyrdom. One by one, men left their cars to see what was holding up the flow. Back and forth. One crowd leaving, one returning. Baba wore a face of ultimate calm, like we were cruising at ten thousand feet, clear skies. I remembered his flight experiments that always proved we were in control. *What do you think would happen if we lost power now?* he'd ask hypothetically. *Say we go through a cloud and the carbs freeze. Would we drop like a rock or glide like a feather? Whatever I answer, he doesn't say whether I'm right or wrong. Hold the stick, he says as he slides the red-buttoned throttle all the way in. The prop slows to a purr. The nose sinks. Earth. I pull hard on the controls. Don't fight it, he says without intervening; Go with it, let it fall.*

Here on the ground, there was only one question: What will I do if they take him? That it didn't come up meant the answer was dire.

Winstons flared up all around us. Smoke rising from dangling arms. Between drags, adept fingers counted prayer beads. Traffic still not moving. A conversation of sorts was taking place through the open car windows, but no one was addressing anyone directly. We were all looking ahead.

"Maybe there's a demonstration up there," someone said.

"Demonstration this, demonstration that," said another. "Okay already. We get the point. I've got six kids to feed."

"It's the will of the people."

"They're burning it all up."

"There's nothing left to burn. They've burnt it all. A nation with raised fists and soot on its face."

"Maybe there's a hanging," someone piped in with derisive cheerfulness.

"For all this delay, there better be."

No one dared respond. The revolution ran on blood. Heads were rolling.

Now somebody cut loose and peeled into the opposing traffic. The approaching cars veered madly to avoid a collision. The crazed driver was bolting for that empty pocket right before the rise in the road. I was watching a suicide. Tons of mangled steel, fragments of skull and guts. But the disaster didn't occur. Up and over, he'd made it! People ran back to their cars and followed suit. Soon, our side of the road had completely overrun one of the opposing lanes, and traffic was no better for it. "Unbelievable," said my father, shaking his head. "This is what our country has come to."

There were many unbelievable things. But were they *true*? Watching my father go about his days as though nothing had happened, as though the revolution was simply a nuisance, was to say home was still home. Revolutionary people were the same old folks, just a bit rankled. Meanwhile, the TV, radio, and newspapers made you think we were caught in the vortex of a great storm.

Unlike at any other time, the last years of the shah's reign were vexed by social turmoil and violence. Charged by the period's ethos of armed struggle—by the examples of the IRA, PLO, by Che Guevara and Castro, by the scathing riots that shook France in 1968—militancy was on the rise in Iran. Guerrilla groups decried Western capitalism, the dependence created with consumerism, and the steady loss of traditional values. Since 1970, three hundred people had lost their lives to acts of terrorism, and with car bombs that targeted American military personnel, the regime raced to show control. The public trial and execution of several opposition figures had the unintended result of radicalizing the entire political spectrum; in the aftermath, you were either a pro-government chum or an antiestablishment extremist. The ongoing debates over democracy or reform or even the meaning of Iran's nominally *constitutional* monarchy were wiped off the table. Substantive change would come only when one person could point a finger at the king and still stand. The exiled Ayatollah Khomeini called the shah "a U.S. serpent whose head must be bashed with a stone" and knew that he'd either come out of it a martyr or a hero—or a tool to those who thought the endgame between the one who was "sign of God" and the one "ordained by God" would free the political process. Somehow, people assumed that after defeating the wicked emperor and his evil empire, the turbaned superhero would recede into his underground hideaway.

The shah perceived dissent as an invasion of ideologies. Marx was strictly banned; Thomas Paine was seditious; Khomeini's sermons about an Islamic government were illegal. He paid little attention to the battle for the heart and soul of the nation. The court, the dominant class, and indeed anyone who looked to the West as a model believed in modernity's self-evident superiority. Who would want to give up a twentieth-century life? Could anyone conceive of women surrendering their right to vote or choosing to be forced to wear a veil? Was it even possible that the judiciary would abandon law books for the Qur'an? How was an arcane cleric who'd devoted a lifetime to the exegesis of a religious text capable of assuming leadership of a country woven into the economy of the West, a state that in the 1970s single-handedly accounted for a quarter of all U.S. arms sales?

In January, the front-page spread in the national paper made every outlandish notion conceivable: a teary-eyed king boarding a jet, a loyal general kneeling at his feet. The headline read, "Shah Gone." For us, for anyone committed to the structure of the military, the king's departure was a devastating blow—the commander in chief conceding to a thin-necked, mustached civilian. But bowing out to a National Front candidate could hardly settle a year's struggle. Clerics and the bazaar class sided with Ayatollah Khomeini. An intellectual cadre backed the Communist Party. And a half-dozen splinter groups saw this as their chance. By February, the revolution had crushed any vestiges of a government, the National Front prime minister had gone into hiding, and Ayatollah Khomeini had laid claim to it all. It was then that the killings began.

Televised court trials introduced us to turbaned judges and foregone conclusions. Familiar personalities defended themselves. Some caved in, pleaded. As a counterpoint to Islamic justice, other postrevolutionary programming stressed the suffering of the shah's foes. Grisly documentaries about Evin, a notorious prison for "politicals," replaced my nightly fix of *Laurel and Hardy*. Ex-prisoners came from all walks of life. "There, right there, they tied me down and ripped out my teeth," slurred a toothless middle-aged man, accusing shah-era secret service agents of acts that made me wince. A younger man with flowing hair like one of the Bee Gees described "the black box." "They wanted me to give 'em names, you know, people I worked with, the ones who told me what to do, but I didn't know anyone like that—I was working at my uncle's dairy store. Sure I complained. We all complained. I couldn't even buy a beat-up car. Back and forth, solitary, pushing a broken bottle in my face, they smashed my thumb with a hammer, see? And then this"—he revealed a marred patch, the size of a coin, off-center on his abdomen, and a second wound on his back—"this is what happens to you when you're hooked to the box."

The voice of the commentator came on louder as the camera zoomed in on the man's face. "Can you describe the feeling, Brother?"

The man's eyes dropped, no words, just the rustle of the camera crew and a pale green wall.

Evin required no commentary, just a jittering camera poking into one darkened cell after another. The cavernous echo of slamming steel doors. Padded rooms with no windows. Shiny surgical tools arranged on a black-topped table. A chair with cuffs for ankles, wrists, and head. Rows of hospital beds. "Yes, dear viewer," said the announcer, "this is the hell we've emerged from."

Was this the plight of the average citizen? I wondered. In and out of Evin? Complain about the price of tomatoes and you get your fingers smashed? At ten, it was clear to me that I belonged to a class with means. The inequities were never hidden. Privilege was a fact of life. And while I knew *I* was nothing, it was painfully evident that I still commanded respect. I'd try to convince myself there was a reason I was swinging a tennis racket rather than racing around collecting balls. Maybe entitlement had something to do with the way you spoke, walked, or looked; maybe it was because your hair was soft, limp, and partable. But then you'd see a silk-haired servant or an official with nappy hair. Now I faced the horrifying prospect of a system devised to keep us safe and privileged.

A year earlier, it would never have occurred to anyone to ask why the gardener, chauffeur, or cook did what they did. But with Evin, every burdened social stratum could perceive itself a prisoner. They had eviscerated the shah's government. What now stood like bars between them and their imagined utopias was the class they'd served.

One evening, while the womenfolk and I struggled with the atrocities of the imperial regime playing on TV, Baba stormed into the living room. "How can you listen to such *charandiat* [absurdities]?" he said. "These are paid frauds who'd say anything." He ordered us to turn the television off, and I felt the same shame I saw in Grandmother's face.

"Who are paid frauds?" I asked a few days later during one of my afternoon jaunts with Baba. It took Baba two beats to recover the thread.

"Actors. They make you believe things that are untrue, and they get paid for it."

"Are all actors frauds? Is Shirley Temple?"

"No. But certainly those bound by their professions to tell the truth—reporters, documentarians. We'll let Superman slide, even though he's a reporter. But no one really thinks he flies, do they?"

"No," I said sadly. I was secretly holding out hope that mankind would someday find Kryptonite.

"Or Herbie the Love Bug. No one thinks he's a living car?"

"No!"

"It would be fraudulent, in fact, if I got on the news and claimed I had evidence, hard facts, that a Volkswagen Bug had a beating heart."

Enough said. Superman amounted to a silly bodysuit. I did not want to follow this trajectory too far. But the conversation helped me understand something: There were things that were true, and things that were untrue but compelling. In the end, we were left to decide *how much* to believe.

With Evin reduced to a movie set for the time being, I began to question the most devastating facts on TV. I even joked with Grandmother that I could fake deformities better than the ex-prisoners we saw. "You wanna see?" And I shuffled across the room. "They wrecked my knees in the awful knee machine," I mumbled. "First this one, and then they popped my right one. I can't even begin to tell you how it felt. I swear to God."

Mamman Ghodsi giggled nervously. "Don't say blasphemous things, my soul."

"That's just it! I really *can't* tell you how it felt." I laughed and laughed.

Some afternoons, when Baba was away and the coast was clear, Mamman Ghodsi would turn to me, press an index finger to her nose, and tune in the trials. We were ready to shut the TV off as soon as we heard footsteps or keys or the front-gate buzzer. Mamman Ghodsi sat at the edge of the couch, biting her lower lip. I sat next to her, matching her intent gaze, not sure what was being said but fully grasping the power shift and what it meant for us. The clergy had coined an unintelligible Arabic label, *mofsed fel arz*: their verdict. I couldn't believe it described us, this foreign phrase

10

scrawled on rectangles of paper, dangling from the necks of the guilty. Morgue shots of the executed displayed the signs on their bare chests, paper softening on skin, ink running with blood.

The trials weighed on me, made me doubly culpable. I was a societal disease, now a disloyal son. I desperately wished to confront Baba, to say I knew things I shouldn't, but to do so would betray Mamman Ghodsi's trust.

"What is *mofsed fel arz*?" I dared to ask my father one day, hoping he would see the question for what it was, my confession.

"Arabic gibberish," he said. His dispassionate tone was the same he'd use if I had asked what an altimeter was.

"But what does it mean?"

"The ending, *fel arz*, means 'of the land.' *Mofsed* is a person or thing that furthers *fesad*."

"What's *fesad*?"

"*Mofsed, fesad, fased, fasada*." Often, my father forgot my generation didn't study Arabic. Since my birth, the country had tried to expunge the language of the Qur'an from our tongue. Those in power thought that Arabic had corrupted our Farsi.

"I don't get what it means," I had to admit.

"Corrupter. It means 'corrupter of the land.' Corrupt, like spoiled. Like to spread rot. It's the bad apple in the bunch that turns all others, the one that attracts flies, encourages stench and decay. If you listen to them, you'll conclude that anything new is a disease, a corruption of the old. We're to go back to outhouses and cholera. To dirt roads and wagons and a perpetual cloud of dust."

Clearly, I'd hit a nerve. Baba wasn't answering me anymore; he was rehearsing a defense.

During this time, regularly, Mamman Ghodsi's eldest brother, Uncle Dear, visited us, ostensibly to check on his sister. His arrival threw everyone into a frenzy of dusting, fussing, and pastries. It was the only time I felt normal during the revolution, connected to a life I'd known, however pathological it was to race around a ravaged city searching for kiwi tarts, éclairs, or napoleons. Uncle Dear would arrive wearing one of his strange but dapper three-piece suits, carrying a bouquet in one hand and his hat and umbrella in the other, always poised with an unctuous, carefully metered line like he'd memorized it.

"How insensible of me, arriving with mere miracles of nature before the Creator's masterpiece!" he'd announce majestically, catching sight of Mamman Ghodsi in the doorway.

Grandmother had an arsenal of cloying comebacks. "*You, Brother Dear, are a twinkle and dance to these weary eyes.*"

With tea and pastries and questions of health out of the way, Uncle Dear turned to my father, the real reason for his visits.

"General dear, do you not suppose the exigencies of history warrant less conspicuity?" Uncle Dear's speech was as antiquated as his Hitler mustache. Almost always, he punctuated his sentences with a couplet from the fourteenth-century poet Hafez, or an unintelligible French aphorism. Through my father's responses, I'd learn what he had just said.

"Hiding, respected dear Uncle, is for the guilty. When one has served one's nation proudly, one should demand attention," my father declared.

Uncle Dear laid claim to a vast swath of Iran's turbulent history. He had lived through not only the rise and fall of the shah, but that of the shah's father. He had seen two world wars. For him, the demise of men was tied to shifts in the times. The whim of international players. Economic maelstroms. One social class sighting another in its crosshairs. Uncle Dear could recall how his own mother and father had squandered the family wealth, gambling. What gold and silver remained, he stored in his basement. The family joke was, Uncle Dear had survived his six wives because he didn't want them to inherit the two candlesticks he'd been left.

"Behold! The most noble of all chests. A resplendent emblem of national pride and glory. But picture, my dear, how in mayhem a scant letter omitted, one man misapprehended for another. Can you fathom the tragedy? *Paris sans 'a' est PRIS!*"

"Fate has had many opportunities to take me out," Baba said with a chuckle. "And I'm still standing." He was the only one who found our situation in revolutionary Tehran humorous.

As far as my father was concerned, whim had no role in the tides of history. Things happened because you planned for them, because of hard work and persistence. It was no accident that Baba was the youngest major general in the Imperial Iranian Air Force. Iran had assembled the most feared air defense in the region, and caprice had nothing to do with it. Why were Iran and America such close allies? Why was Iran the only country America entrusted with its most sophisticated fighter jet? If you asked my father, he'd say this was all the result of toil, dedication, and strategic alliances.

Maybe I personified the nation: He poured his love and energy into me with such intensity that, as I looked back on my young life, I saw a seamless merging with the man I called my father. We attended the first day of kindergarten together. We inspected military hardware together. Together, we did homework.

"Penmanship starts with your own shaped quill," he explained to me over one calligraphy assignment, "not some Bic or even a fancy fountain pen." He gathered half a dozen stalks of bamboo, then cupped his hands around mine and showed me how to whittle. "Take off a small sliver at a time. See? You have to will this thing into life, convince it of its new, noble role." In his caring, persuasive hands, the stick and I were both convinced.

"Here's the mouth of an *N* exactly three dots wide," he'd say. "Look at *H*—not just a lifeless loop, but the marvelous shape of a pregnant woman. Think of *J* as the upper lid of an eye. Make it a dark, flirtatious eye. Can you feel it flirting with you? Now center a mole on her cheek. Gorgeous!"

More than what he taught, I studied my father. Whenever Baba and I drove anywhere, I had a hand on the steering wheel. When we flew, I memorized his input through our linked controls. Nightly, when he sat at his desk to authorize requisitions, we reviewed everything together, line by line, my eyes following the exact stroke of his swan-shaped signature.

"May I try that?" I asked once.

"What?" he said.

"Signing."

He thought about it for a moment and handed me the pen.

"Do we approve of the purchase?" he prompted.

"Yes," I said. "Don't they need tires?"

"They do."

So I did the most natural thing, as I had practiced it a thousand times in my room, steady and sure—a stepped line, a short dash, and the swan's upswept wing.

"Remarkable," he murmured under his breath.

It was hard to tell where my father ended and where I began—and what of us, if anything, could survive this revolution. But the crusade threatened more than one man or boy; it rejected fundamental assumptions. Did we have the right to claim stewardship of a nation? Was my mother right in holding us to a higher standard, in requiring a certain sensibility that was patently ours? And my greatest torment: What of Bubbi, my villager nanny? Bubbi, the one who bathed and fed me. Bubbi, the face I saw every night as I fell asleep. She was part of my life the moment I registered thought. Did she and I now fall on opposite sides of a line set ablaze by the revolution? The oppressor and oppressed? Could we still be friends?

* * *

On one after-school outing, my father and I took an expressway westward toward Shahyad Tower, the most conspicuous structure in all of Tehran. Baba wanted to drop in on a poultry farm he had funded. On the way, he briefed me on the details of the acquisition—the partners involved, shares, amounts owed. Maybe he missed the briefings he used to give before each flight. Maybe the end was closer than I thought.

"You have a twenty-five percent share in this farm," he told me. "Your brother has another twenty-five. My sincerest apologies— up until recently, you were both in debt. We didn't even know if the chickens were going to make it."

Shahyad loomed in the distance, a diffuse enigma. The structure sat in the middle of an immense square onto which many roads converged. As you approached it, it grew taller and taller, crisp and white against a deep blue sky—*Look what Iran can make!* it said. The monument was our version of the Eiffel Tower until the revolution renamed it Freedom Tower; henceforth we would pursue freedom *from* modernity.

The expressway we had taken ran along the edge of the city, its path marked by rolling hills to the right and the city skyline on the left. At one point we came to a stop at a traffic light, the intersection free of traffic. The few stray buildings to which the crossroad led did not seem to warrant a light, and certainly not on a major artery. With the car humming quietly, my father facing ahead, I looked to the right and followed the path. It wound up to buildings partly obscured by arid hilltops. The landscape reminded me of our desert air force base. I was instantly drawn to it. How strange, I thought, that I had never noticed these hills, so close to Grandmother's house, yet so hidden. How placid the bare land. I wished the light would never turn. My father and I could leave the car running and walk away, climb the tallest hill. We'd sit together on top of the world, safe from the country's woes.

"Baba," I said, "where does this road go to the right?"

A deliberate moment passed before I heard the reply.

"To Evin," he said, quietly shattering any illusion of a past to which I could return.

"Corrupters"—it was all I could think about. But when I thought of the people around me, their indiscretions yielded nothing but irony. My mother's sister, Aunt Z, was notorious for her irreverence, yet she was the most pious Muslim you'd ever meet. Bubbi, with her genuine fear of Allah, was his greatest aggressor. And the one whose blood this revolution sought to spill—you would be hard pressed to guess his crime.

Did people really want to go back to wagons and outhouses? I thought of creaky carts in *Bonanza* and *Little House on the Prairie*, how distant that world seemed compared to the one in which I'd lived—supersonic jets as long as I could remember. Picturing outhouses took even more imagination. My father often used the word, giving my mother reason to poke fun at it. We would all laugh. Now the utterance made her nervous.

"Here we go again," she said. "*Outhouse*! Who says 'outhouse' anymore? Do you call a train 'smoky machine'?"

"What should I call it?" asked Baba.

"Washroom, like everyone else."

"Very well. Washroom," he repeated agreeably.

"I mean, really!" My mother's entire way of life was under assault.

"What's an *out* house?" I asked.

"Happy now?" she said to Baba.

"What? I don't see the catastrophe," he said. "In my time there was no plumbing or running water and, so, no indoor facilities. People dug a deep hole in the corner of their yard, stuck a room over it, and called it an outhouse."

"Note the past tense," she inserted.

"Could you see, I mean, was it all there in the open?" I asked.

"Let's just say you wouldn't want to read any books on the potty."

"Yuk!"

"What, you think that's bad? Where do you think our water—the water we drank!—came from?"

"I don't know."

"There was a little canal that ran in front of all homes, connected to other canals that stemmed from the north side of town and ultimately from the mountains. The canals were normally dry except when the city directed water to your neighborhood. Every few weeks ours would run, and then it was an all-night affair. The water would arrive at the head of the neighborhood and feed the houses there first. Then the next house. Then the next house. You had to stand outside and wait your turn. When the house up from you was done, they'd release their dam and you'd be next, ready with a paddle-shaped thing to stick into the canal to flood it, to divert the flow into the trough that led all the way to a room in your basement—the water storage. In the basement, on the base of one wall was a spigot where you could then draw water."

"You drank ditch water?"

"Well, after you'd let the critters and things settle first."

"Live bugs?"

"Sure. You could see them wiggling around."

"That's gross."

"What's gross is that in the summertime kids would sneak into the water storage and splash around."

My mother added her own story, to counter Baba's, but her background was marked more by tragedy than glory. It was true that her grandfather and great-grandfather had been courtiers, but theirs was a lost era. Compared to modern statesmen, they were comedic: Great-grandfather's court title had been "Extraordinary

Among Nations." Of the extraordinary wealth he *didn't* leave behind, his penchant for gambling, and weakness for women, legends loomed.

"My father, bless his soul, had the freshest stream water *delivered* to the house," she said. "It came in a huge metal container on the back of a wagon, and the men filled our tall, ceramic pots, which lined the patio. It was called Kingly Water."

"We had kingly bugs in our neighborhood," Baba said with a snicker. He wasn't proud of his past, but he recognized it as the starting point of a colossal journey that had brought the country to the here and now.

Whenever he talked about life as it had been, he prefaced his remarks with "in my time," and for good reason: My father's time had vanished. There was no other way to conjure it. There were no coffee-table history books to flip through. No museums to chart the transition. No antiques markets glorified the knickknacks of a bygone era. "In my time" meant malaria, cholera, and typhus. "In my time" meant Baba's father started coughing one day and was dead in a week.

Without doubt, it was the stubbornness of one man, the shah's father, that brought Western modernity to Iran, replacing the dirt roads of Baba's childhood with paved streets, Jebreil (the angel Gabriel) as an explanation for death with medical diagnosis. Reza Shah's swift military victories against separatists, his dissolution of five hundred years of Turkish rule, his unprecedented turn from commoner to king set the tone and pace of the changes that came with his rule. The early twentieth century held vast promises, which Reza Shah embraced with fierce conviction.

Plumbing, sewer systems, electricity, public transport, train tracks, hospitals, schools, universities, a court system, banks, surnames, all blossomed overnight. For people used to wagons and outhouses, the changes were dizzying, alienating. They instilled in my father the most fundamental assumption of modern times: Nothing stood in the way of human achievement but lack of will.

Reza Shah wasn't some calcified figure out of an old, dusty history text; to me he was an enigmatic character from a storybook whose chapters my father repeated like bedtime tales. "Once, he was inspecting the kitchen of an army barrack. Everyone was on edge; they knew that when Reza Shah inspected something he *inspected* it, none of this 'We love you, we're loyal, therefore we're doing a good job.' No sir. He'd look in the cupboards, pull out drawers, wipe the floor. Picture the kitchen staff sweating bullets! So he comes to a large cauldron in which the day's soup is being made. He picks up the ladle and starts stirring. Up comes a bunch of things—potato, lentil, meat, knucklebone—the kinds of things you'd expect. But then this blob surfaces. He pokes at it, turns it around, studies it, a dozen other heads leaning over the pot. The thing barely sinks before he pulls it back up. Identify this, he says to the cook. The cook can't."

By then, I'd heard the story a million times, but I couldn't wait for the punch line. "What happened then, Baba, what happened?"

"He threw the cook in the pot."

"Why, Baba, why? Why would he throw the cook in the pot? Oh, that would hurt. Wouldn't it, Baba? Wouldn't it?"

"Yes it would. He was saying it doesn't matter who you are—king, cook, vizier—you have a responsibility to your position. How could you not know what went into your own soup? What if the blob were a shoe? What if your kingdom was invaded and you didn't even know? What kind of operation would you be running?"

With that same headstrong drive, my father commanded his air force base. If something stood in the way, he dealt with it, right then and there, repercussions be damned. Once, when Baba and I were driving around the base on a late afternoon, we overheard the control tower on the radio. The scratchy voice of an air traffic controller reported a mysterious obstruction on one of the runways. Baba reached for the handset. We would check it out, he said. "Take us there," he told me, and I steered us from the passenger seat to the airstrip.

"What do you think it is, Baba?"

"I have no idea."

"Why did they call it mysterious?"

"Because they have no idea either."

"Could it be a flying saucer?"

"At this point in time, we have to leave all possibilities open. So, yes."

"A *flying saucer*? From outer space?"

"Sure. Why not?"

Our flying saucer was, in fact, a long black snake, stretched across the runway, basking on the hot tarmac. We circled the creature and came to a stop near its tail. My father got out of the jeep and, unwisely I thought, approached it, expecting the snake to slink away. Nothing. Man and beast studied each other a long time, neither budging. Finally, my father broke the tense silence. "Do you have clearance to be on the runway?" he said to the snake. No response. He nudged the thick mass with the tip of his shoe, and I gasped. Patiently, the snake straightened, the sun flickering on its slick back. More probes and prods. More adjustments from the snake. Baba climbed back in the jeep, aligned it with a few acute turns, and drove over the snake's head. Driving back to its tail, he lifted it inside, closed the door on it, and drove off.

I couldn't believe what had just happened. A black stub rested next to Baba's thigh, and he gazed ahead, business as usual, like we were a couple of seasoned snake catchers.

"Is it dead?" I wanted to know.

"Let's hope so," he said.

Wind through the jeep's flapping plastic windows rustled the snake, and I couldn't be sure the creature wasn't struggling, thrashing about, arcing its head toward us to do whatever awful thing angry snakes did to people who drove off with them. At home Baba sauntered into the house, and the servants crept out, horrified. "Oh my God!" one of them whispered. "What's he want us to do with it?"

Anything was possible in my father's universe.

2

Breaking the Sound Barrier

My father's stratospheric rise paralleled the nation's rapid ascent. Key to both was the establishment of free public schooling. Of course, it wasn't as easy as that. State-sponsored education overlooked the fact that families relied on their children to get by. But Baba's mother was no ordinary widow; despite staggering hardships, she saw the potential in my father and resolved to see him through his twelve-year education. And the state met its side of the bargain. The graduate was versed in French and physics, classical Persian literature and chemistry, calculus and Hemingway. Next stop: Tehran's new Air Force Academy. Then to America for flight training, Germany to fly the first series of jets, and England for Officer Candidate School. In Germany, Baba was recruited as a jet instructor for other NATO pilots, and this opened the rest of Europe to him. A few years later, he was back in Iran leading the Golden Crown aerobatic team. Squarely placed in the jet age, here was the same boy who, twenty years earlier, stole rides on a donkey-drawn wagon in the dust cloud of Tehran's unremembered streets.

For an Iranian to be at the forefront of anything, a lot needed to have happened. Reza Shah may have been a catalyst, but the groundwork for change was laid by the generation preceding Baba's, a brand of influentials whose faith in modernity bordered on religious zeal. So passionate were they, even the most learned cleric of the turn of the century gave his blessing when the parliament pushed for a first constitution: "We don't know what this *constitution* is," he said, "but we're willing to try it." Two decades later, in the 1920s and '30s, Reza Shah's transforming dictates made the new an indisputable tool of prosperity. By my time, an entirely new culture had taken root. It was a given, for instance, that Uncle Norooz would sneak in with toys on New Year's; that birthdays would always be celebrated with the birthday song, cake, and candles; and that there had been a tooth fairy all along. But things had been much different for my parents. For half his life, my father had no idea when he was born, and never knew about the ritual of "making a wish" when blowing out candles. Only when he was in his twenties, when his mother made an offhand remark about a snowy day in April, was he able to pinpoint his birth date in a farmer's almanac. My mother had experienced *her* first birthday party when she was eighteen, which indicated Grandfather's savvy in employing "modern practices" to showcase his marriage-age daughter to a house full of men. No other mechanism, besides a suitor knocking at your door, allowed a sanctioned social space for young adults to meet face-to-face. Certainly, my mother's uncle's pilot friend from the poor end of town would never have had a chance to talk to my mother.

Although I wasn't aware of it, deliberately I was allowed to lead an unencumbered childhood. I could question anything, challenge anyone, and the adults of my youth reveled in my audacity. A child's freedom was the hallmark of the new. Baba's early lessons targeted assumptions. For a year, when I was four, he ordered Bubbi to delay my bath time so that he and I could bathe together at the end of the day. He would enter the bathroom in his swimsuit, and we'd make a mess with the foam, the splashing, and the flying toys. We'd also conduct hydrologic experiments, working with balls that frustrated all my efforts to keep them down, or upside-down jars that refused to drain as I raised them.

One night Baba pushed a big bowl underwater, facedown. I was to guess what had happened to the trapped air.

"Are you sure the air is still under there?" he asked me as he kept even pressure over the bowl.

"Yes," I said recklessly.

"Then you should be able to stick your head underwater, lift it inside the bowl, and take a breath. Agree?"

I saw where this was going. "Maybe," I said more cautiously.

"Maybes won't get us anywhere. Give it a try. See if your theory is correct." He said this with absolute neutrality.

I went under, raised my face inside the bowl, and against all my instincts, took a deep, abiding breath.

The man required a commitment, and I handed myself over. I did this because he, too, was committed; he gave me his all. On his arrival for the occasional lunch break or his return in the evenings, I would leap onto his back and dangle from his head and shoulders. He seemed content with a monkey on his back. Reading the newspaper. Conversing with guests after dinner. Helping my brother with homework. Omid was eight years older than I, and he tolerated me with the air of someone who had not had the same privileges in his own youth. But he wasn't resentful: It felt as though we were on the cusp of a historical shift, that the very idea of a child was shifting with me. When Baba had an official phone call, I nested quietly on his head. Seeing Bubbi enter the room with a tea tray, I'd squeeze my father's head between my knees, take the cup for him, and feed him.

Bubbi's piercing black eyes routinely fixed on mine. "Get down from there," she hissed. "It's boilin' hot."

"Don't worry, I know what I'm doing."

"You're gonna scald Agha, I say! Get off."

"I'm careful."

"In the name of Allah, merciful and compassionate, get down!"

"I've done this two thousand million times."

Bubbi countered, "Akh! Someone's gonna get hurt. Come, I said it. God's witness. My soul's at rest. . . . You'll mangle Agha's mouth, I say. Ehh!"

In all of this, my father was invisible. If he were going to be scalded, it was out of his control. Who was he to quell my enthusiasm? In his eyes, I was the very force of life—curious, eager, heedless—and he loved to see me in my element. I could do anything, it seemed, and he would be my willing accomplice. The only boundaries I faced were imposed by my mother, who had to choose her battles carefully: If her reasoning seemed to falter, I would take the matter up with Baba, who would dissect the issue ad nauseam.

My brother, Omid, was harder to usurp. The culture placed great import on the eldest son, and our military setting heightened this sense of filial rank. But before he was sent to a London boarding school, his rightful status was constantly undermined by my insults. My mother had devised a strict seating arrangement around the dining table to crystallize our roles: My father sat at the head of table; she always to his left; Omid to his immediate right—the so-called deputy position; and I, next to Omid, farthest from Baba. She had also limited our Coca-Cola consumption to one glass but neglected to restrict trades. Thus, dinners for me presented an opportunity to taunt implicit hierarchies.

"How would you like a sip of my Coke?" I'd ask Omid.

"How big?" he said.

"Down to here." I wiped sweat off my glass, a line just above the ring of painted cherries.

"How many laps?"

"Three," I said.

"Two," he countered.

"Okay, two, but you have to gallop."

"Excuse us a minute," he said, and I climbed his shoulders in the middle of dinner for two trips around the living room. If I couldn't sit next to Baba, then neither of us would. And if it wasn't Coke I bartered, then it was a spoonful of ice cream, half a tart, or anything else my mother placed limits on. Or it was by sheer attrition that I drove everyone away from the dining table, keeping Baba to myself. There was a certain chemistry between us. I'd ask questions for which there were no ready answers, and he'd stun us with his sober theories before anyone had a chance to concoct some second-rate explanation.

"Can things ever fall *up*?" I wanted to know one night.

"Sure. Gravity is the attraction between *two* bodies! Which is why the earth is constantly falling up, toward you. It pulls on you and you pull on it. Of course, I'm pulling on you too and you on me and we on Bubbi and Bubbi on all of us and so on. Give us enough time, remove that pesky thing called friction, and we'd all be stuck together."

"Really?"

"Really."

"Will you all have to come to school with me then?"

"Either that or you would all have to come to work with *me*."

"Why are leaves green?"

"They absorb all the colors in the visible spectrum of light except green, the one they reflect." He considered his own words. "Funny how we should be recognized by the attribute we reject, isn't it?"

"Is the tooth fairy real?" I asked him.

My mother quickly interceded. For weeks she had been hyping the coming of the tooth fairy, and with my first loose tooth hanging on by a thread, she wasn't going to let Baba ruin her hard work.

"Of course he's real," she said.

"How come I never heard of him then?" I asked her.

"Because you haven't lost any teeth," she explained reasonably.

"Did he come for you and Baba?"

"Sure! The tooth fairy visits all boys and girls."

"Did the tooth fairy come for Bubbi?"

"Bubbi skipped that step, my love. She went straight to adult teeth and bitterness."

When I asked Bubbi about this, she couldn't remember her first tooth, but she was sure no fairies visited her. "I never heard of no such devil, creepin' by dark, breakin' into innocent people's homes. I'll wreck his mother-bitch mouth if he tries it with us. You wait."

When I lost my tooth, I studied it in the flat of my palm. It was either true that a tooth fairy existed and I was inviting a stranger to violate our home, or the whole thing was a strange, profane hoax.

The morning after the tooth fairy's scheduled visit, I opened my eyes to an exquisitely wrapped box on a chair next to my bed. It was my mother's work, I knew: the understated but festive wrapping paper, the snipped edges folded neatly before being taped down. A handmade bow topped it all—loops of multicolored ribbon, each cut obliquely on end. I was confronted with a choice. I could acknowledge my mother's handiwork, or I could accede to the new. I chose the new. I ran around the house screaming that the tooth fairy had come.

By 1975, flush with oil cash and eager to propel Iran to the ranks of military heavyweights, the shah had decided to purchase a fleet of new fighter jets. For a year, Iranian Air Force officials had been courted by the United States Navy, Air Force, and Marines, who showcased their latest air power in a bid for the Iranian market. The shah had been given a green light to buy anything he wanted. Any interest on his part would have meant hundreds of millions in sales. In the end, the F-14 Tomcat won. Its weapon delivery system was unmatched by that of any other fighter jet; it could shoot down an aggressor a hundred miles away. Baba was put in charge of the project and the jets' new home in Isfahan: Khatami, Eighth Tactical Air Base.

My mother and I spent the summer before our move to Khatami in London, settling my fourteen-year-old brother in at his new school. The base was still being built, and my mother couldn't bring herself to deposit my brother in a foreign land and leave. Every Friday, she and I would take the train to his countryside home situated among graceful, intensely green hills and lush willows. The three of us would return to the city for the weekend and go back, two days later, along the same scenic path, which had somehow lost its Friday allure: Now the greens seemed jarring, the weeping willows sad, and the school itself a stone penitentiary with tiny Gothic windows to lock my brother in. When we left him for the last time, Omid walked the length of the train-station platform waving forlornly. He looked stunned and betrayed. I plastered my face and both palms on the plate glass, and my mother gave in to silent paroxysms that lasted all the way home. Whose idea was this? I wanted to ask. I was seven and wondered if this would happen to me someday.

By fall, our house on the base was finished, and we moved in. It was a sprawling house, which felt even bigger without my brother. We arrived months before the planes for which the base was constructed. A palpable sense of pointlessness permeated everything, everyone: big house, but no one to share it with; vast swath of desert turned into an air force base, but no planes. I was to start second grade with the Americans in the city, kids whose parents had come in support of the F-14 project and for the nearby Bell Helicopter plant. When the Americans took their two-day weekend, I would attend the Iranian school on base.

When the jets finally arrived, completing their cross-globe journey, raking our sky with their thunderous roar, the mood lifted; we had a purpose. Up close, the flying machines looked much less menacing. Their glass canopies looked like big soap bubbles. I watched my father take delivery of the first batch of planes and shake hands with orange-flight-suited American pilots, who were a good foot taller than anyone around. There was no denying it; America was a giant. It was the most technologically advanced country in the world, the most dazzling, the most talked about. And here we were, giddy over a squadron of F-14s adorned with our own insignia and khaki camouflage; after all, no other nationality had been allowed to set foot in the plane. Some viewed exclusive, superexpensive jets as unnecessary and wasteful, especially when the nation was struggling to send its kids to school. But I felt my chest throb each time I heard a tight pair of swept-wing Tomcats screeching overhead—or as Bubbi liked to put it, ripping the sky's ass apart. I felt a direct link to the jets, to the base, and to the crisp salutes we received every time we drove past the kiosk at the head of our driveway.

The base soil, a salty desert, was inhospitable to most plants. When several experimental, salt-tolerant species shriveled up, my father ordered the removal of one cubic meter of dirt every twenty meters along the main roads so an imported soil could nurture the flora of our imagination.

"What kinds of trees do you like?" he asked me.

"I don't know, big ones with lots of branches," I said.

"But leafy ones or conifers? Ones with fronds or the traffic-cop cacti you see in Westerns?"

The saplings that finally survived looked like ragged old brooms stuck handle-first in the ground. But they were lovely scrags, grateful to have been given a chance. Harnessing the earth's potential was no small matter. The concept, called *abadi*, stirred the Iranian soul, even if opportunities to better the land were scarce. For my social class, its most common expression was lavish inner-city gardens, or orchards on summer properties on the slopes of Tehran's mountainous north. The quaint agricultural land belonging to one of my great-uncles, which he rented out under feudal agreements, was nothing more than a gesture. In truth, even those who actually lived by the land—two-thirds of the nation's population—were slowly being robbed as industrialization drove them to the cities. However imperfect, trees in the desert quenched a collective thirst for *abadi*. My father named a "tree-planting day" on the base, and for the opening ceremony, we gathered in suits, ties, and patent-leather shoes to stab shovels into a mound of chocolate-brown dirt and feed saplings to an audience's applause.

Minor miracles begat major ones. Frequently, before supper, I joined Baba on his various inspections of the base—to gauge security at a missile bunker, to check on a road repair, to see about a new, house-size generator. The most curious drive we took was to a far-flung corner of the compound, a few acres being carved by a half-dozen busy bulldozers puffing black smoke. The end of the paved road meant little to Baba, who stopped at nothing to satisfy his curiosity. At first, my interest was in the drive itself; I steered the car, and it was fun to maneuver around potholes and boulders. But as the bare land sloped deeper and deeper, as its peculiar shape started to impress itself on me, my interest in the surroundings grew.

"What are they doing?" I asked finally.

"Digging," said Baba.

"Would they come out in China if they kept on digging?"

"I think they'd end up in . . . Texas," he said, pausing to suggest he was calculating latitudes.

"How long are they going to dig?"

"Long enough to remove two meters of dirt."

"Is that a lot?"

"It's enough so that when we fill the void with water, the level will be over our heads."

"Where're we going to find that much water?"

"Another excavation is doing just that."

When all was said and done, when the floodgates were finally raised and water rushed to fill the massive hole in the ground, we watched a lake come to life. Within a year, the oasis welcomed ducks and wild geese. A fringe of cattails sprouted along its banks. More surreal was waterskiing in the desert, made possible by the reservoir's careful shape, which absorbed wakes left by a speeding motorboat.

I was awestruck by my father's magic. What he dreamed came to life. Two identical guards manned the entrance to the base, two stood outside our driveway, two with matching white spats marched around a rotary, and two German shepherds arrived in crates one day to guard our house. Seeing the base through Baba's lens made me part owner of it. I wanted to show him that I under-stood order and uniformity. One summer, I spied on drivers I sus-pected of speeding. My older cousin kept his dirt bike at our house, and for the task, I helped myself to it. But the motorcycle was too tall for me and difficult to stop when I caught an offender. Instead, I was forced to take notes in motion, a compiled list of license plate numbers, dates, places, and times of violation, which I submitted to Baba with all the seriousness of the officers who made nightly appearances to give him progress reports. He looked at me quiz-zically, seated behind a tower of paperwork. After reviewing the document with extraordinary care, he thanked me and praised my effort. "Very thorough!" he said.

For my next sting, I chose the kiosk guards. I'd overheard my father complaining to the guards' commander that the sentries placed at either end of our half-circle driveway left their posts and cackled together "like a couple of chatty schoolgirls." One afternoon, I noticed the sentry manning the kiosk was missing. I rushed into the house and into Baba's study to get a good vantage point. With the curtains slightly parted, I saw the man gabbing with his partner at the other end of the driveway. That evening, as soon as Baba arrived, I related what I had seen to him. He turned and left the house. It took a minute to realize what I'd done and why he'd stormed off. I ran back to his study and tore at the curtain to find him on the street, wrenching the guard's ear, roaring in his face. The soldier fell to his knees. I felt light-headed and nauseous, then hot: Baba would have to return and resume the role of father instead of my commanding officer; the man would have to get off the ground and assume the look of a dignified soldier; I had to pretend to be a kid.

My father's unwavering trust in me was frightening. His questions were serious. When he asked me what I thought about a car of my own, I knew it wasn't an idle offer. At four, I had been entrusted with the wiper blades on our drives—I could turn them on and off whenever I deemed the windshield dirty. Then came the horn. At five I had a hand on the steering wheel whenever my father drove. Now the steering wheel was exclusively mine. I had even begun to commandeer the accelerator from the passenger seat. My forays into driving were immeasurably empowering, for when my father put his trust in you, he receded, even if collision with light poles or fire hydrants seemed inevitable.

One morning, before school, I asked if it would be all right if I got his Bronco ready, and Baba consented. "Sure, have K give you a hand."

Mr. K was one of our drivers. He was short, stocky, and spry eyed. His nappy hair and creamy-brown color marked him as a *shomali*—a northerner, one of the "port people" of the Caspian Sea. Mr. K's stunted arms and legs suited his peanut head, notable for its close-cut shave. But it was a perfect head: soft facial features, petite nose, miniature ears the size of mine. However, the man's manner was anything but exemplary. He was recreationally bitter, defensively inimical, always fearful he was losing ground to Bubbi, who'd ride the staff just to let them know who was boss.

Following me out of the house that morning, the driver struck a feckless pose; he didn't care what happened to my father's car. He had just been told he was no more useful than an eight-year-old.

Bubbi's blare trailed me as I stepped into the biting cold. "Where you going like that? Move what damn car? You'll catch chest 'n' side and croak. Come, I said it. You wanna croak?"

So my first drive, with a quietly vengeful Mr. K slumped in the passenger seat, took the form of a forty-foot jog from one side of the driveway to the other. We turned the heater on for my father and left the car running with a shaft of vapor pumping out of its tailpipe. I stood there shivering and grinning.

More elaborate strategizing to get behind the wheel ensued. Once around the driveway. Down the street and back. When reports started to filter in from the MPs that the general's Chevrolet Impala had been spotted on back streets, apparently driving itself, my father accepted that I was unstoppable. He would need to get me my own vehicle lest my career as a car thief really begin to take off. We spent months considering various options—a go-cart, a motorized rickshaw, a Japanese minivan with wheels the size of a wheelbarrow's—but none impressed Baba. He considered them "toylike." "What you need," he asserted, "is something with guts, something original." Finally, in what seemed like a fantasy, he purchased Uncle P's VW Beetle, tore off the body, and, with the help of a hired welder, undertook the task of making me a dune buggy.

While the car was being stripped, Baba told me to fetch my favorite toy cars. He asked me detailed questions about the features I liked most. In penciled sketches, he pieced together my imaginary car. "What do you think of a roll bar? We can give it an airfoil shape to minimize drag." Many drawings later, and after months of drilling, sawing, and welding, a car materialized in the backyard.

To say that it was unique is an understatement: The seat backs held fuel; the seat belts were remnants of a C-130 that had crashed; intake scoops presumably cooled the engine in the rear; the car was free of doors and windshields; and my mother painted a black octopus on the sheet metal forming the forward wind deflector.

The octopus was a curious choice. Behind my mother's back, Baba threw me a wink, signaling me to let it slide. My mother had worried about her grade-schooler owning a car; trusting her with the hood design was bound to earn us her support. I would have chosen a bird of prey—an eagle, a hawk perhaps, or something like the falcon my brother once brought into the kitchen.

It had been an unforgettable event, one of the few clear memories I had of my brother at home. Omid had started high school in America and was back for the Christmas holiday. When I saw him, *if* I ever saw him, he was madly dashing. Dating three women at once. Hunting. Horseback riding. Working on his pilot's license. Twisting nights away at a disco. My parents seemed to regret the family distance they'd caused by sending him away, and the freedom was his payoff.

I was on a routine run to the kitchen for tea and biscuits when I noticed the falcon perched on the edge of the kitchen counter. I stopped dead in my tracks, unable to make sense of an enormous bird looking on as Bubbi stirred that evening's stew. Bubbi was ill-disposed toward birds and, by association, all flying things. You might even say she deplored the air force itself. Yet here she was, sharing her kitchen with an angry-looking bird. With a glower, she explained that "our friend is a present from the big hunter man," a reference to my brother. Omid could do anything, it seemed, even crash our Chevy Impala or invade Bubbi's kitchen with impunity.

But with the falcon, he'd taken things too far. Birds of prey were objects of reverence, appearing in folklore, proverbs, and in one form or another, on all air force uniforms. That the general's son had wounded one was an unfortunate and delicate matter.

"How could you do that?" I asked him.

"It was so high, I mistook it for a crow," he rationalized.

"But you can't eat crows." I was invoking one of two rules my father had set with guns: Eat what you kill, and do not aim in the direction of people. The first rule was the reason Bubbi was reduced to making sparrow soup and blackbird stew, and why the kitchen was not a good place to be before these suppers. She'd curse and deplume the carcasses in sharp, exasperated yanks. By the end, she and everything in her wake would be covered in a fuzz of feathers.

Eventually, Omid revealed his true motives in a hushed, furtive tone. "Don't make a scene. I'm having the falcon stuffed for Baba. Wings spread, swooping. Think of it! In his office. It'll be great."

The bird sat on the kitchen counter for two days, its wound tucked out of sight, waiting for the arrival of the only person on base who knew taxidermy and who happened to be on leave. It sat tall, blinked indignantly, and studied our movements with an unnerving precision. No one dared tell my parents of the bird's presence. Since they never veered into the kitchen, the bird continued to haunt us.

Then on Wednesday it was gone.

"Bird's a goddamn bird, staring at me with those wretched rooster-anus eyes," Bubbi said. She had swept the bird into the trash can, closed the lid, and left it out on pickup day. "Its mother was a dog," she offered shrewdly.

So birds of prey had a special significance and would have been a fitting tribute for my own loyalty to the air force. But apropos of nothing, my mother had chosen an octopus. Anyway, the design was a trivial matter. The Iranian culture has a pronounced dimension of worry and ill prediction; add to this a kid driver and a mysterious contraption and everyone foresaw disaster. Baba assured them there was nothing to be concerned about, that I would only be allowed to drive when I'd been "properly certified." I could see their eyes pinwheeling. What the hell did *that* mean?

I began a training regimen modeled after flight training programs. After school I'd log time on the "simulator," which amounted to the car running off the ground on four jack stands. Periodically, my father observed these sessions with intensity, watching my ghost shifting as he would a jet pilot throttling up in a tight turn. Next came actual drives, preceded by briefings in the dining room where a toy car modeled our exact path from and back to the driveway. Baba and I suited up in helmets and gloves and navigated the remotest streets, never leaving first gear. This was almost worse than hovering in the driveway pushing levers back and forth; I knew how to drive and the baby steps were excruciating. No arguing with the general, though. "Any dimwit can drive! *Procedure* is what you're learning," he explained.

Fifteen sessions of sheer boredom opened the door to second gear, which was more exciting than any New Year's gift or birthday present, especially since this phase coincided with emergency maneuvers. I'd get up to speed and my father would call out imaginary obstacles—pedestrians, cars, a stray dog—and I had to swerve or screech to a stop without killing the engine or the pedestrian. In these runs, the desert turned into *The Streets of San Francisco*, and Baba and I were a couple of cops chasing bad guys. Debriefings back in the dining room reintroduced the realities of the desert, the air force base, and my age. We practiced other drills until sunset, supper put on hold, the base personnel watching as the commander and his son navigated the streets in reverse, parallel parked between imaginary cars, executed three-point turns pointing them homeward, and drove away backwards.

My final task was to show proficiency in pop-starting the car, and it didn't count if I simply navigated. No, my father required that I help push the car before jumping in to start it, making sure I didn't end up under the left rear wheel. Out of our driveway and up the street toward the main road, Baba killed the engine where the pavement flattened.

"Imagine you've lost your starter and I'm someone else," he said.

"Let's pretend you're Mamman Ghodsi."

"Fine," he said. "As long as Mamman Ghodsi isn't called to push."

Before I decided to find help, I got a good sense of a car's weight as I tried various schemes to get it rolling. Nothing. Pushing with all my might moved the car three inches, and as soon as I stopped, it rolled back to the starting point as though an invisible magnet were at work. I soon learned that pop-starting a car required as much social as driving skill. How do you convince a gardener, a soldier, or passerby to leave what they're doing and to help an eight-year-old restart his car? When my assembled crew showed up to get me going, they noticed my father waiting on the side-walk with his clipboard. The men quickened their pace, growing more and more obsequious. Of course they would help. They were dying to help.

"Mr. Aria," they insisted, "you get behind the wheel and we'll get you going."

"Thank you, it's fine like this."

"Are you sure? Because we don't really need any more help pushing."

"Thank you. It's really okay." There was no way to explain that the general was pretending to be a grandmother, and he wanted me to push.

All at once, the driverless car took off—down the road with four eager men putting on a spirited show of force for my father.

Sprinting! It was all I could do to catch up with the car as it headed for the main road. Catch up and throw myself in. That I managed to start the car was a minor miracle.

When the day of my driving exam finally arrived, I felt it was more for the nonbelievers than me. Short of rebuilding the engine, there wasn't anything I hadn't done or couldn't do. We announced the occasion to the household with much ceremony. Even the kitchen crowd looked on in reserved suspense. Smooth shifts, emergency maneuvers, proper hand signals, driving in a straight line in reverse—all things I'd mastered. When I pulled back into our driveway and parked the car, Baba slid his helmet off, shook my hand, and said, "Better than a truckhand. Consider yourself checked off."

According to Baba, you could take any kid gaga for cars, give him or her training, and instill mastery. I was his proof. Limits were self-imposed. Forget that a kid shouldn't drive, and see what can result. But the lesson wasn't just lost on the staff: Steadily, I was becoming the tool by which my family validated its social place.

To the base kids, the car made me as curious, unexplainable, and wonderful as the first monkey in space. But my skyrocketing popularity also made it impossible to make friends. Other eight-year-olds stuffed little plastic flaps in their bicycle spokes to make the sound of a motorcycle; I chased speeding motorists on a real one. They had to put their toy cars away before dinner; I had to remember to park mine in the carport for the night. Once, when the shah's nephew visited us on the base, I was allowed to drive him back to the city in my car. It was the only time I had driven off the base—his driver in the car behind me, my driver in the car ahead. Thursdays, when the base school ran a half day, I'd drive to my only friend's house. Together, we headed off-road—the desert our playground. I aimed for humps that could launch us into space but ended up in a shower of dirt and pebbles. Getting moored in a patch of ash-fine dirt was more exciting yet. My father had strapped a folding shovel to the car, and we took turns digging for better traction. When the car lurched forward, free and clear, we felt like the most powerful eight-year-olds in the world.

More commonly, in our remote setting, village boys ran around with shaved heads and dust-beaten clothes. They were a constant question mark for me. I remembered passing one entire family hanging off a tiny motorcycle. I felt embarrassed catching the eye of a boy, my age, teetering on the foot peg he shared with his siblings, one arm wrapped around his mother.

I often saw them on my drives to Isfahan chasing after an old bicycle tire or kicking a flaccid plastic ball. Like Baba, I wanted to believe we were the same, but I wondered in what universe these kids would ever have the same opportunities I did. Baba had installed an old fighter jet on a pedestal at the main roundabout inside the base. It had a slight bank, a gentle climb, and stood high enough that I could imagine it scraping the upper layers of the atmosphere. He had a second jet, the same model F-86, placed a kilometer outside the base. This one was low to the ground and flew level. One afternoon, we were driving to Aunt Z and Uncle P's house in the city when I noticed a few village boys crawling over the aircraft. I knew there were strict areas on a plane on which one could and could not step, and my instant reaction was of alarm. One boy was riding the canopy. One was walking the length of the fuselage like a trapeze artist. Another was jumping up and down on the horizontal stabilizer. Turning to Baba, I saw the most content smile I had ever seen on his face. I knew exactly what it meant.

My own dreams involved speed. The paved streets imposed rigid limits, and the desert was rocky and uneven. When I took up the issue with Baba, he agreed that speed was a uniquely human preoccupation. "The last great barrier humans overcame was the speed of sound," he said. "When Yeager finally crossed it in the X-1, it changed much more than aviation."

"Have you ever crossed the speed of sound? What happens? Do you think I can cross the speed of sound?"

One day, I was to follow my father in my car. He didn't preface this opportunity with his usual "How would you like to . . .?" It was more of an order, a lapse, perhaps, a rare moment when Baba slipped into his official capacity. I was so excited, I avoided asking any questions. Maybe we were on a mission. Hurriedly I changed into my white driving overalls, put on my helmet and gauntlets, and ran to the carport as though the base's safety relied on me. My father was waiting in his Bronco, sitting patiently behind the wheel of the running car. As I pulled up behind him, he took off without a word. Out the gate. Out onto the main road and toward the central roundabout. Then away from it. A left at the next junction put us on the only path toward the operational heart of the base. Only then did I start to wonder where we were going. My father's regal pace made the unknown more ponderous. The expansive desert turned questions into well-guarded secrets.

At a heavily manned gate, the Bronco crept to a stop. A guard approached my father's window. His arm stretched in and then bent mechanically for the salute. The barrier rose, and my father rolled through. I knew better than to try to tag along; Baba took gate-check protocol very seriously and in his presence it would be observed to a T. I pulled up and stopped. The guard marched out. "Your identification," he said routinely, as if kids driving octopus-adorned dune buggies were a staple of the air force.

I was prepared. No one lacking an air force ID with the proper endorsement could cross, and since I sometimes visited or accompanied my father, a pass had been issued in my name. I held out the card, which had, stapled to the upper left corner, a recent buck-tooth picture of me in a light blue T-shirt that read "Super Kid." It contained my name, my occupation (student), and my rank (general's son).

"Your business?" the guard asked me.

"I'm following my father."

"Does the general know you're following him?"

"I think so," I told the man while Baba idled quietly on the other side of the gate.

The guard took my ID inside his kiosk and got on the radio. "General, this is the front gate, do you copy?"

"Go ahead, gate," came Baba's crackling voice. We could have heard him better had he just stuck his head out the window.

"I have a young man here who claims to be your son. He says he is following you. Do you confirm?"

"Yes," said Baba.

"How would you like me to proceed?"

"Let him through."

And through I went, with a salute intended just for me.

We roamed aimlessly through the ghost town known as the restricted zone. The excitement I had first felt when my father suggested our outing was now a dark, ominous shadow creeping along next to me, snickering. Was this another test? Get me lost in unknown territory and say, Here's a compass. Your next task is to find your way back? Another soldier, this one out in the open and in full battle gear—helmet, canteen, and machine gun—blocked us before we could approach the pair of Tomcats up ahead. I couldn't make out his exchange with Baba, but whatever was shouted back and forth convinced the soldier to lower his weapon and let us by. Some nonsensical security code was renewed on a daily basis and any lack of compliance with its gibberish had serious consequences. To his infinite amusement, Baba had once been held at gunpoint until a minor authority could come and remind him of the day's code.

Leaving the checkpoint, my father and I drove onto the tarmac and past the aircraft. Farther yet onto the runway, the general stopped. He stepped out and strode back to me to say he had frozen all air traffic for an official speed run. I was to go as fast as possible down the runway and record my maximum speed.

Down the runway . . . maximum speed . . . It took several seconds for the words to sink in. With my palms wet, my heart revving, I lowered my helmet visor and taxied to one end of the silky concrete where a U-turn put me in view of a flat expanse dissolving into a sky-blue mirage. A moment's pause and I buried the accelerator. At eight, my sound barrier was 100 kilometers per hour, and as I watched the needle rise to the magic figure, runway numbers, marker lights, and the black streaks of rubber all melded into a rushing, frantic world few mortals had ever experienced, or so it felt. At 110 and 120, the steering wheel began to beat wildly from side to side, the car went into a raging shake, and, as I held on, I could barely register my own quivering.

3

I Raised This One

For all the freedom I was afforded, Bubbi made sure to keep me grounded. There was a whole world in the kitchen, with Bubbi at its helm, that stood in contrast to the way we lived, to our aspirations. Bubbi was so steadfast in her attitude, you were left thinking there was only room for one of us on this earth. "God's answer is coming," she would say, "He knows I never tasted no wine."

She never approved of my car. It wasn't that she thought I couldn't drive or showed poor judgment. Bubbi would rather see a child humbled by respect for adults, for a house, for the earth. Respect for the Almighty. Wanting anything, let alone a car, was insolent. The child never asked—the child was told. But Bubbi's problem with me went beyond my appetite; it involved anything new or unprecedented. Cars were disrespectful of a human's biped nature. Fighter jets were downright demonic. Bubbi disapproved of the way my mother dressed in knee-length skirts and spaghetti straps, of her flowing hair, and her opinions. In Bubbi's estimation, women were crucial homebodies. "Shamefully," the women of my mother's class had careers and made business decisions and imagined new conditions for all women. And then there was my brother who'd always chafed at Bubbi's unbending views. They had given up on each other long ago. The latest problem was Omid's "American" ways.

45

A Don Juan in training, he attracted women Bubbi thought loose and licentious. It didn't matter that the girls came from respectable families or that their dates with my brother were governed by laborious cultural restraints. For Bubbi, romance was dangerous. As for my father . . . He was the patriarch, after all, and Bubbi's upbringing said, Show blind respect. To the untrained eye that's exactly how she was: devoted and deferential, tradition incarnate.

Bubbi was not a phenomenon. Far from it—she was typical of villagers who ended up working for affluent families—an entire Cinderella class without the happy ending. The villager nanny did all the chores, cooked and cleaned, and in return enjoyed the comforts of an upper-class lifestyle. If pay were negotiated, there was the added advantage of sending money back home, supporting an extended family left behind—in Bubbi's case, her son and daughter. If Bubbi was in any way unique, it was because she never wanted to be with us. She would just as soon be with her own kind, in her village, content to live the backbreaking life that produced a block of cheese and a sheet of bread at the end of the day. This was what Bubbi believed. Or the myth she wanted you to believe.

There was one compelling reason to think Bubbi *would* rather go back: the fact that she couldn't. Word had it Bubbi had come to us because her husband had vowed to kill her. Before he could get his hands on her, Bubbi's family had put her on the first bus to Tehran, where she was to stay with a relative till things cooled down. My brother was on the way, my parents needed a nanny, and Bubbi's husband never backed down. So she stayed with us—permanently temporary.

"Why did he want to kill her?" I asked Mamman Ghodsi one day in Tehran, during the revolution, after we had moved in with her.

"Oh, what tall questions, my dear sir. Who wanted to kill whom?"

"Bubbi's husband, he wanted to kill her, isn't that right?"

"Who's to say what's right, my soul? What's done is done."

"Mamman Ghodsi, c'mon, be serious. Did he want to kill her or not? Why would he want to kill her?"

"Why does anyone want to kill anyone? The paper is filled with the dead. Does anyone know why? Who knows, maybe Bubbi lost her head and said something she shouldn't have. Maybe they were a bad match and she flew the coop. Maybe she was running with someone." Grandmother always knew the answer, only it required a jackhammer to dig it out of her.

"Bubbi had a secret *lover*?" It was hard enough to imagine Bubbi married, let alone engaging in an extramarital relationship. The woman was homely.

"My dear, don't get so excited. All I'm saying is that the truth isn't always plain. Our own nanny, God bless her soul, came to me and said Fatimah the Laundress knew a fair girl from her village who needed a place to stay. I talked to your grandfather—he had a soft spot for such things—and we agreed to take her in. Now you're asking me where the onion begins and where it ends. May the peace and mercy of God be with you."

"Did she ever tell you who he was?"

"Are you writing a *roman*, my life?"

My earliest memories of Bubbi were bittersweet. When I was two or three and living on an air base I vaguely remember, my mother enrolled at the university in the city and left me with Bubbi from dawn to dusk. I threw a fit. Routinely, two military privates were assigned to our household, and we hired a third hand—"We need somebody with half a brain in the kitchen," my mother argued. Between sobs, one morning, I accused them of hurting me. My mother was shaken by the news and called them in, one by one.

"Missus, I swear on my mother's soul, there's a mistake. I've never touched Mr. Aria. I'd as soon laugh at my own grave," the first one said.

"And you *will* laugh at your own grave," my mother stressed.

More groveling from the second soldier.

She called Mammad in. "Is it true you pinch Aria when I'm gone?"

Mammad was the civilian servant, less timid than the other two.

"It's true, Missus, that he pinches *me* and *bites* and that I haven't lifted a finger except to put ice on my wounds. Twice, I almost had to have the driver rush me to the infirmary."

And, instead of consoling me as a mother might, Bubbi corroborated his story.

Caught in my lies, I still didn't give up. "They *want* to hurt me. Mammad *wants* to pinch me. And Bubbi's mean to me," I told my mother.

Bubbi scowled at me; no words, just a baleful stare that cut to the heart of my tantrum.

The truth was, it was *Bubbi* whom I yearned to be near and hold. I followed her every step. When she relaxed for a smoke, I seized her, one eye glued to the cigarette that counted down my time with her, drag by dreaded drag. The cigarette put Bubbi in a trance. She peered out the window into nothing. I could have been holding onto a tree stump. At times her heart softened and there was no end to the love she could show. She called me her son and let me hold her, wrapped an arm around me, perched me on a hip as she stirred dinner. Or she put me on her lap and pressed me to her chest and I breathed in her week-old smell like it was the last time I'd be this close to her. But for every drop of affection, there was an equal measure of resentment—of me, my family, the military, the culture she consistently found at odds with her village ways.

Losing Bubbi was a real possibility. Every now and then she blew her lid and, using me as a pretext, rushed to gather her meager belongings. "That's it," she'd say to me as though I had gone a step too far. "I'm packin' my *boghcheh* [wayfarer's sack], and I'm never comin' back. Damned be my pappy's pappy. Who were you foolin', comin' here? Satan kid. Satan in the sky. Better off in my grave." She pretended to leave for her village and then returned, then left again—always for good. It was a nerve-wracking ritual I took for real, crying my eyes out each time, begging and pleading with her not to go. When she did, no one could console me. Once, I decided to follow her. I found her sitting on the ground outside the kitchen with her back against the wall. It soothed me little to know this was the most Bubbi could manage: It didn't change the fact that she had left me. Maybe she'd sit there forever. Maybe when I'd come back to check on her, she'd be gone.

When I was older, I used any excuse to be in her kitchen. I tried to teach her to read and write. After homework, I took out a fresh sheet of paper and began my daily harangue. "Look, here's a *B*," I said with as much enthusiasm as I could muster. "If you just do this one letter, you can write *half* of your name!" Bubbi cast an incredulous look in my direction as though I'd just asked her to touch her big toe to her nose, and she turned to her work without a word. But I was persistent. "Look, *B, B, B, B, B* . . . I just did a hundred of them, which means I could have written half of your name fifty times. Look how easy, *B, B, B, B, B* . . . here's ten more. C'mon, just try it. I'm sure you can do it!"

One day, she set down her ladle, wiped her hands on her apron, took a seat at the kitchen island, and stared at the piece of paper as though it were a well and she the one who had decided to jump in. Holding a pencil for the first time in her life, she struggled to follow my example, wincing and pursing her lips and fighting to form a stepped line and a round dot. It was heartbreaking to see her like this, to stare at the heavy, meandering scrawl she produced. I wanted to hold her and cry, but I controlled myself.

"That's great!" I said shamelessly. "I would definitely call that a *B*. And you even gave it a tail."

Not one to fall for empty praise, Bubbi turned on herself. "You laughed at your pappy's beard, you wench. *You? Write?* Stick to what you do best: cleaning the shitter."

Bubbi hailed from Sabzehvar, a town in northeastern Iran, in the state of Khorasan, a region of mythical significance to the ruling class determined to connect with its pre-Islamic past. Khorasan was thought to be the home of Iran's settlers, the Aryans, the same Slavic race that later inflamed Hitler's imagination. The most famous Khorasani was the tenth-century Ferdowsi, a poet whose thousand-year-old national epic was routinely enacted as the most authoritative voice of our lost past. Iran had been scarred by the ravages of many invasions throughout its history, but none was as disfiguring as the Arab/Islamic conquest. Under Arab conquerors, the indigenous language was outlawed. In turn, Islamic cosmology supplanted native stories. Ferdowsi's collected tales offered a glimpse into who we were, or at least who we had been, before Islam.

How the boorish Bubbi could have come from such a hallowed place was beyond me. As far as I was concerned, if you were from Khorasan, you were a distant relative of the heroes and heroines of Ferdowsi's epic. A handsome copy of Ferdowsi's book held a prominent place in my father's library. Pictured on its cover was the Archer.

"Do you know Arash the Archer?" I once asked Bubbi as she skinned soaked chickpeas. I thought she must certainly know the legend.

"Huh?"

"The Archer! The one who saved Iran by shooting an arrow all the way to the Oxus River."

"Whose kid is he? I don't know no river like that."

"We were fighting Turan for years and years, and they were destroying us, taking all of our land," I said. "Maybe they got tired or maybe they were done, I'm not so sure, but they decided to stop. They said one of us could shoot an arrow in their direction and where the arrow fell would be the new border. So the Archer came and shot his arrow, sheooo, and it flew all day and night like to China or somewhere really far. And that's how come we beat them."

"I never heard of no bow 'n' arrow man," Bubbi said. "And don't be using no sling or arrow round the house. You're gonna smash a window, and then who's got hell to pay? Me, that's who. Like I don't have enough goin' to watch over windows."

In truth, Bubbi hailed from a kitchen—the *real* heart and soul of Iran—and ours was her official domain, a command post from which she ruled the servants with a Stalinesque harshness. She spied on them, interrogated them, promoted them, or banished them to the laundry room with an iron and a bottle of starch. The kitchen of an Iranian house was much more than its counters, sink, and stove. It was the home's hub, a crossroads in which the servant class met to climb the intricate social ladder, to buy and trade things, to gossip and complain, to make merry, or to feast.

The kitchen was such a world unto itself, governed by its own rules, that my mother discerningly had gone on a campaign to bar me from it. She perceived personal relationships with the soldiers, servants, chauffeurs, gardeners, and villagers who had suddenly ended up inside the barbed-wire boundaries of our air force base as an invitation for disaster. And the reason she always gave, my mother's winning card, was "private body parts."

"Yours to see, no one else. Understand?"

"Not even Bubbi?"

"Bubbi's okay."

"What about Baba and Omid?"

"What kind of question is that? Father, brother—they're the dearest people you've got. What possible interest could they have in your *story* anyway?"

"I don't know; you're the one saying other people want to see it."

"I don't mean your father!"

"How about the guards?"

"Definitely not. No guards. No men in uniforms. No men at all."

"No colonels either?"

"No! Are you listening to me? No men. Absolutely no men. Majors. Colonels. Not even the commander of the air force. Get it?"

"What about my aunties?"

"They're okay as long as they're helping you. Say you have an emergency, you just can't hold it, and we're not around. But not if out of the blue they say, Sweetie, let me see your *story*."

"Auntie Miriam says she wants to taste my fresh grapes."

"She means you're adorable."

"I don't think Bubbi wants to clean me anymore. She says she's either a cook or a butt wiper. Not both."

"Don't worry about Bubbi; I'll deal with her."

"What about Uncle P?"

"This isn't twenty questions. The only thing you have to worry about with Uncle P is his foul mouth, not his hands."

It was true that Uncle P was inordinately fond of the phrase "pussy-giving sister," using it to describe reckless cabdrivers or anyone else who irritated him. In Uncle P's parlance, even inanimate objects like a blunt knife or a radio that wouldn't tune in a favorite station had loose sisters. But why I should or shouldn't worry about his hands was baffling. Moreover, why anyone would have any interest in my excretory processes was beyond me.

I Raised This One

Despite my mother's fear of molestation—her ostensible reason for class separation—some sort of collision was guaranteed in the person of Bubbi. She belonged to the proscribed group, and my sanctioned interactions with her opened the door to the rest of the illegal class. And this wasn't the only loophole that undermined my mother's idea of a sequestered and class-appropriate childhood. A greater challenge came from my father, who truly believed there was nothing inherently superior in anyone. Even himself. Presumably, the servant who was stuck with the chore of serving us tea or the gardener who toiled under the searing sun lacked one or both of two things: resources and will. The combination could turn you into anything, regardless of your background. The semiliterate Reza Shah had proved it.

In the kitchen, where I loved to pass time, I had to tread the very fine line between heedlessness and smugness. In forming friendships with the staff I defied my mother, and in being standoffish I let down my father. The target class faced its own problems. Chumming with the general's son gave the impression they were upstarts, that they thought of themselves as social equals. On the other hand, failing to return my goodwill made them disrespectful of the general's son. And God forbid if there was any question of wrongdoing. My father had left such a bitter memory with Chubby that everyone walked on eggshells around me.

Years earlier, when my brother and I still shared the same house, we owned an ill-tempered pet Pekinese, "Chubby." In the course of two years, Chubby had scratched my cheek and bitten Omid's lower lip, and each time my mother had defended the dog. "Why were you blowing up his nose?" "And you, the older, supposedly wiser brother, feeding an animal from your plate. *Under the couch!*" Chubby's last outrage had turned the day into a frenetic drive to the base infirmary and finally to the hospital in the city. But it was all for naught; with or without stitches I'd have scars where the dog had bitten me. When Baba returned home in the afternoon, he knelt in front of me, on the porch, and examined the tower of gauze taped to my mutilated cheek. His aching eyes ran over my face as though the details of the event were all there to be read and felt. He said nothing.

Before he went inside, he told one of the soldiers to fetch some rope.

Out again in plainclothes, Baba tied Chubby's hind legs and flung the loose end of the rope over a branch of the birch in the front yard. Up went the dog, a dangling piñata, the gathered staff taking positions behind the door or window from which they gazed in horror. My mother was the only force who could have intervened, but in her absence we watched, helpless, as my father buried his belt in the animal whose deranged squeals left a permanent mark on the onlookers. Later that evening, when she found Chubby panting hoarsely on his side with bloody welts and one popped-out eye, my mother lashed out at us. She called us savages: I was the savage who tempted the dog; my father the savage who beat him; and it was savagery to watch the beatings without protest.

Far from making me feel safe, this loose-gun side of my father added paranoia to my burdened household relationships. What if Baba thought someone had crossed a line with me? To what extent would I be responsible for the hanging that was sure to take place?

Even so, I found myself drawn to the kitcheners, to their alluring stench and slur. In the real world of real people you could drink Coca-Cola out of a bottle recycled so many times all the high points on the glass had chafed white. You could buy bread from the locals who lived in the clutch of mud houses down a winding dirt road. The steaming miracle they fished out of a hole in the ground—their oven—had a thin layer of dust and soot, which made it better than any bland white baguette. French feta was similarly dull;

local cheese hinted at goat and chives. The list went on. Slippers with cartilage soles. Little round felt hats encircled with a ring of salt where sweat had dried. Crisscrossed legs in front of a hookah. Bizarre delicacies behind a deli's curved-glass refrigerator—heart, brain, tongue, tripe, grilled stomach, liver. The impressions formed a picture of a tantalizing world closed to my own breeding, and I was hopelessly smitten.

The eclectic crowd in the kitchen, a labor force that came from all over the country, had its own appeal. They were the lowest-ranking members of the air force and the most minimally educated cross section of society you could ever meet, completely unaccustomed to the military or to urban ways. They were taught to be invisible, to blow in and out with a tea tray, to whisk away the empty glasses and return them full. "Never say nothin' to no one," Bubbi instructed them. "Serve from the right. Don't bumble the order. The general first. Then the missus. Don't linger out there like it's your aunt's house. Move your ass. You spill on the doily and I'll shoot you myself." None were as harebrained as we imagined them to be. "So where are you from?" I'd ask one. "Where is that? Can you draw me a map? Do you have any brothers or sisters? Have you ever driven a car? Ever been to a cinema? Who do you think will win the World Cup? Did you go to school when you were growing up? What will you do when you get discharged?" And the answers were fascinating. It was my country's tale I was hearing, in different dialects, curious inflections. Some gesticulated; some were grave and stone-faced; some were kind or kooky or grumpy. My overwhelming impression was that they were incredibly sure—the same quality that made them seem ignorant to some. I loved every second of their utterances. They didn't proselytize or push Truths. You had to ask, and when you did, you'd succumb to envy: They knew everyone in their town and everyone knew them; their mother, father, sister, and brother were their greatest assets;

you had never even seen the likes of the peaches, persimmons, or quinces in their orchards; the river running through their hometown was the most idyllic body of water imaginable.

Mammad, the full-timer, was the only conscript who had ever stayed beyond his mandatory two years. He habitually stole gasoline from my father's Bronco, cut deals with the gardener, ran a healthy black market with the driver, hawked military equipment with the locals, and was always on Bubbi's good side for the tithe he offered her in cartons of Winstons. The only time he faced expulsion was when my mother discovered he had called in the base carpenter to shave the legs of two Italian armchairs to match the uneven parquet floor.

"Have you eaten donkey brains?" my mother asked rhetorically, staring at the hobbled chairs.

"No, Missus. Why?"

"Because only a donkey-brained imbecile could have thought of such an inane thing."

"Have you tried them, Missus? They don't wobble anymore."

"Of course they don't wobble! Now point one a quarter turn away and it's a goddamn seesaw."

"Why turn them, Missus?"

"Get out of my sight. Pack your things and get out. Go! And don't set foot in this house again."

It wasn't that easy to get rid of Mammad. Whether or not he was donkey brained, the kitchen wouldn't be the same without him. He was an outlet for the staff, and the kitchen was his theater. When the show was on, they gathered to watch him astutely mimic all our guests. Except for my parents, no one was immune from these sketches, with the higher-ranking generals and stuffier socialites getting encore performances. One moment Mammad was a mighty military man shouting ridiculous orders at the kitchen crew. "Boy, you get your ass up that tree and start crowing like a rooster. What? What's that you say? Roosters don't crow in trees? Who do you think you're correcting, cabbage head? I'll have you hung by your ears. Six months in solitary! You'll spend the rest of your service doing the crow's leap." Then he would morph into Mrs. Hoity-Toity. "Bubbi dear, be a sweetheart and grab the end of this dried mucus and remove it from my nose. No, not that nostril, this one, this one."

Bubbi did not risk losing her authority with such horseplay. "Get lost," she'd snap.

"But darling, I get so light-headed when I imagine the awful substance. And the dreadful thought of it in *my* nose!"

"I said get lost, ehh!"

With his pretend English, the jester would switch to an American specialist with lessons in wiping or polishing or dusting. "No, dis vay, dis vay. Loook, *d-e-e-s* vay. Kileening kileening kileening, no half pass nine. Vat time it is? Faster goood. Faster faster."

A favorite prank of Mammad's, and something only he was capable of, was rousing our miniature poodle. He would kneel next to her, point at something, whisper in her ear, and the dog would charge—a fluffy, white, growling torpedo. When he turned Poodie loose on the commander of the air force, Mammad's prestige soared among the kitcheners, who thought of him as their most daring, bold, and irreverent brother.

Just as you couldn't tell where the next soldier would come from or what talent he would bring, you couldn't be sure of his social standing. Conscription applied to rich and poor alike. My mother's driver, Ab'bas, the spitting image of John Travolta, was socially elevated. Broad shouldered and trim, he moved in graceful, feline strokes as though each swing of leg or arm showcased a craft, each turn of head a purpose. But there was no sense of conceit—you might just as well begrudge a fig beetle its electric green color as

Ab'bas his radiant green eyes. In the man's lavish presence you became part owner of his playful grin and irrepressible charm. When he and I weren't throwing a volleyball back and forth in the kitchen—oh, the munificent compliments he'd lay on me for a good dig or a spirited hit—Ab'bas mesmerized the kitchen crowd with tales of his latest serendipitous run-in. They swarmed around him like moths to a lightbulb and listened closely as Casanova recounted his adventures in the city, pausing to take quiet, deliberate sips of tea.

"She checked me out from the start and I did one of those, you know, like, I got your number but I'm too busy to ring just now. You should've seen her, boy, auburn hair halfway down the curve of her back, big hazelnut eyes, lips like you've cut a peach open. She was wearing a headscarf. Around her hips! And I mean tight, boy, like, Here you go, here's your present. I'm saying to myself, Oh my God, the missus is waiting at the hair salon and I run into this? So I'm sitting there thinking of excuses—Sorry, Missus, had a blowout, got into it with a traffic cop—and I hear this soft clop-clop, look over my shoulder, and there she is, staring right into my eyes. Wouldn't you know it? She wants directions! 'Forgive me,' she says in this tulip voice, and I'm like, *Forgive you?* I'll give my neck for you."

"The devil," one of the bumpkins let slip.

"You're doin' us dry, man, go on, what happened?"

"Well, as it turned out, she didn't need directions." Ab'bas would never finish his fabulously charged stories. He only crowned them with a coy, sideways glance.

"Shut your traps!" Before objecting, Bubbi would first listen to the whole story from her high stool in the far corner. "Worthless bulls, all of yous. Don't you have nothin' better to do? Standing around, finger in butt, sayin' sin. Go polish some trays," she'd bark at the privates. "Ab'bas, why don't you go tend to your pansy-mansy ways outside? Go comb your mane or somethin'. Go on, the lot of you."

I loved to take my breakfast in the kitchen, on a bar stool next to a gurgling samovar, looking out over a rusty desert coming to life in the morning's quiet before anyone else showed up and Bubbi turned adversarial. Each day, tensions started to mount whenever Mr. K stepped in and uttered an intentionally vague good morning. Bubbi took this as a personal insult, and as Mr. K took a seat at the end of the counter, requiring tea, she'd walk over to the steaming samovar, lift the chimney, and empty a pot of cold water into the urn. Sorry, no tea till the water comes to a boil again. This set the tone for the rest of the day, the kitchen a fabulous battleground between the two proud warriors.

In the car, Mr. K exhibited a double life I had come to accept as part and parcel of life. Mornings, on the way to school, past the base's exit gate, he'd turn to me with a mischievous grin, reach down underneath the dash, and expose the tape deck he had spliced into the car's radio. Sliding his favorite cassette into the stereo gave us jangling "port music," a sound as discordant as the wailing of the Gypsies we'd sometimes see on our drives into the city. They donned faded black rags, made bonfires in empty lots, and pounded their bare feet to the clanging of pots and pans. Meanwhile, buses sped past them and glass buildings towered above their heads. Mr. K and I shared similar split existences: He wriggled, swayed, and snapped to sappy love songs, and I gazed over placid fields of poppy.

There were a few thousand Americans in Isfahan, and by the time I entered fifth grade, we had moved to a dedicated campus with sports teams, school plays, sock hops, and yearbooks typical of any primary school in America. As one of only a handful of Iranian students, I experienced school as a bizarre cultural affair. It felt like a daily, round-trip flight to a foreign land. From the time Mr. K deposited me at the front door of the building, I had mere minutes to become a different kid, a disadvantaged outsider whose class and clout meant absolutely nothing. No one seemed to know who Baba was, and no one cared. With time, I had grown to like the anonymity: My mistakes didn't cast a shadow on our family; I didn't have to question whether some accolade wasn't in fact a nod to my status. Last bell transfigured me back into the general's son, a minor authority at eight, feared by those who had glimpsed the unbridled love and trust my father reserved for me.

Bubbi's morning slight had an answer by the afternoon. When Mr. K and I returned home, he would pop the trunk, stroll into the kitchen, and order one of the soldiers to fetch the groceries.

The pile of bags set Bubbi off. "What are these eggs for?" she'd mumble. "We haven't touch't the two dozen from the other day."

Mr. K smiled. "Are you saying I just decided to buy more eggs? Do you think I've got a thing for eggs?"

"I got enough cabbage in there to make borscht every night of the week. Meat to feed you all kebab for a month. Turnip like I got a bazaar stall. I don't need no more eggs."

"Look here, the missus gives me a list, says get this. And I get it," said Mr. K. "If she wants a chicken coop full of eggs, that's what I get. I'll get her the damn chickens that laid the eggs if she wants."

Bubbi's face would turn twisted, and she would start blaring. "What am I gonna do with thirty more eggs?"

"Take it up with you-know-who."

When calm, Bubbi was still an unpleasant sight, owing to the pockmarks and large hairy moles on her face and to her mismatched, floral village wear. Year-round, it consisted of baggy pants with elastic cuffs and waist, a long skirt, an apron, a long-sleeve shirt with rolled-up sleeves, a sequined vest, and a head scarf. Whenever she served tea to my father in the morning, two of the most disparate forces in our society stood together in close proximity, incongruent in every possible way, fiercely holding their respective grounds. They were the only two people who got up before the morning sun. They spoke few words, and I wondered if there wasn't some underlying fear of defeat for the one caught unawares.

Iranian villagers exhibit a certain private harmony, which is sagely attractive. You could dismiss it for its indolence, for its pride in the face of the new, but somehow even I registered its benefits. Refusing to sleep on a real bed, shoveling rice into her mouth with coned-up fingers, hand-washing and line-drying her clothes every other day, preferring silence over music, frowning on possessions, barefoot and bold—this was how Bubbi lived. I was eight when I first wised up to her view of the world. Bubbi and I were seated outside on the steps leading to the kitchen, peering at an immense, desert sunset, listening to the crackle of burning tobacco as she took slow, long drags from her unfiltered Camel. To my family, inactivity, especially in camaraderie with a shiftless, "backwards" villager, was illicit. But I learned that the pleasures of life were essentially uncomplicated. Bubbi *let* me see this.

One sweltering summer afternoon, as the air-conditioning worked to cool an empty house, I pushed open the kitchen door to find Bubbi, one of the servants, Hassan Agha the gardener, and two of his men sprawled around a big wooden bowl on the floor. It wasn't uncommon at noon to find a bunch of laborers waiting outside the kitchen door; each day, Bubbi fed lunch to the extended crew. Sometimes a couple of them mustered enough courage to nod when Bubbi asked them if they wanted seconds. Seeing how they stood paralyzed behind the screen door, she'd call them in, "Well, don't just stand there like you got a stick up your butt." And they'd slither in and wait near the entrance, their eyes glued to the floor, respecting the home's privacy. It was safe then for me to ogle them: their mud-caked shoes, mended pants, faint traces of a floral-print dress shirt under heavy creases, stains, sweat, and manure.

That summer afternoon, I would have dismissed the strange gathering in the kitchen—it was miserably hot outside—were it not instantly clear I was viewed as the trespasser. The way the laborers' eyes rose to mine showed no shame or admission of indiscretion. Rather, they seemed indignant, just as criminals feel entitled to their privacy while committing a crime. I'd carved a unique place for myself in the house that allowed me to cross class and cultural divides. Now, suddenly, somehow, I'd lost my cover and landed on the wrong side.

Frozen in the kitchen doorway, I robbed half a dozen faces of their smiles. Finally, Bubbi intervened. Squatting on the kitchen floor, she stretched an arm to me and said, "Come here, my son," and then turned to the others. "This one's all right," she said. Bubbi's greatest gift was to erase me from time to time, to wash me clean of labels.

The bowl held *abdoo-khiar*—thin yogurt with raisins, cucumber cubes, walnuts, sprigs of mint, salt, and ice. I walked over and plopped between Bubbi's crisscrossed legs. She began stuffing my mouth with scoops made from torn-off pieces of flat bread. The men's quiet stares told me they were unconvinced. It wasn't until the ladle came around and I sucked hard like the rest to keep yogurt from running down my chin that the heaviness lifted. They broke out laughing. "Didn't I say?" said Bubbi smugly. "*I* raised this one." The more I struggled with the ladle, the more we laughed. It was a markedly different kind of laughter than I was used to. No one had said anything clever or insightful; no one had revealed a cultural double standard. We seemed to be bellowing because we could, just as it was satisfying to slurp and gulp and produce a loud

"Ah." Surrounded by such earnest, tear-filled eyes, by their gaping, gummy smiles and crooked teeth, I felt happier than I'd ever felt.

These interludes continued haphazardly; sometimes Bubbi would gesture to the staff that I was not to be trusted. Sometimes she was more liberal. But somehow I always felt that when push came to shove, Bubbi would forget our differences, and I'd be *her* kid.

4

Where Parallel Lines Cross

"What is corruption?" I asked Mamman Ghodsi. I desperately needed a counterpoint to Baba's sangfroid, and Mamman Ghodsi struck the perfect balance between bewilderment and hope. Finding her alone, reading the paper for the third time, shaking her head over the latest executions, was strangely comforting: Terrible things *were* happening; I was right.

"I beg your pardon? Were you talking to me?" she said.

"Mamman Ghodsi, there's no one else here."

"You mean no one left! Corruption, my soul, now has a religious meaning. It refers to acts against God or against what the mullahs call sharia, meaning God's rules."

"Does it sometimes not have a religious meaning?"

"Well, last year it didn't. And who knows what Fair God has in store for us next year."

Questions regarding God were perplexing; they revealed a deep crack in society. But lately, those same questions, and the same dissatisfying answers, made the difference between life and death. Half of us, it seemed, were God-fearing Muslims. The other half were God-evading modernists. For the religious crowd, Islam was only a starting point: More importantly, they were Shi'a, whereas the vast majority of the Muslim world were Sunni. Given that Shi'ism was homegrown, it was possible to be Shi'a and patriotic. The secular crowd saw things differently. Shi'a meant Islamic, and Islam was an impediment to change and prosperity, to international currency. The world, with America as its poster boy, was blazing ahead while the pious were stuck knee-deep in religion. No one argued that Shi'ism wasn't an Iranian construct, but it never sat straight with modernists that Shi'a's Islamic roots were a product of the Arab invasion some thirteen hundred years earlier. Adding twelve hundred more years to our Islamic calendar (as the shah did in 1976) made us heirs to an un-Islamic past. It was then that the Persian Empire reigned over a great territory spanning across North Africa all the way to China's edge. Winding the clock from 1355 back to 2535 meant we could shrug off the legacy of defeat. It meant we could draw from all that had made us great and would do so again.

The pious/secular crack cut through society in unpredictable ways. My mother, starstruck by the glamour of Paris, Rome, and New York, was secular. Her sister, Aunt Z, was religious. Their father, Baba Vali, had been a fierce modernist, while their mother, Mamman Ghodsi, took pride that she could trace her ancestry to the Prophet Mohammad. But Mamman Ghodsi was hard to place: Though she was deeply respectful of Islam and the twelve Shi'a saints, she was decidedly unorthodox, looking to God first and then to God's messengers.

On the family's other side, my father's mother, the one everyone called Mother, epitomized Shi'a orthodoxy. In contrast to Mamman Ghodsi, with her floral dresses, cheerful lipsticks, and Soir de Paris scent, Mother never went without a headscarf or a chador. When my father was a schoolboy and the shah's father banned Islamic garb in the name of modernity, Mother was stopped once by a policeman who tore off her chador—denuded her, as she thought, in public. In the shah's time, it was admissible to wear anything you pleased. Women traipsed around half nude in their short shorts, but Mother and her chador were inseparable.

Her commitment to Islam was a tool that got her through life. Her faith made her a tough woman, *khaki*, or "of dirt"—humble yet proud. When my father's father died of pneumonia, Mother depended on Islam to raise my two-year-old father and his three siblings. When she was permanently handicapped after a fall that shattered her pelvis, she became even more praiseful of God's many gifts. She prayed and fasted; gave tithe and visited the two holy shrines in Iran; and she made it the centerpiece of her life to care for the needy—in massive proportions. Regularly, a stream of poor people came to her house to eat, and Mother was all-obliging. You would never have guessed from the outlay that a struggling widow stood behind all that generosity. On her visits to our house, I tip-toed around her, afraid that I might offend God if I offended her, fearful of her piercing gaze and her unnerving comments. "Scrub those teeth clean, my dear," she'd say to me at night, "or else Satan will piss in your mouth."

In contrast to Mother's, Bubbi's piety came in phases. There were great stretches during which she showed no religious leanings at all—her venomous words eclipsed any wrongdoing I could be accused of. And then she would turn to God, rote and ritual. But her bid for piety was never convincing. The nasty, vulgar Bubbi was the one you could trust. When she went on one of her prayer binges, I'd hide in my room anticipating her noontime worship. I'd wait until she was fully engaged to crawl out from under my bed or pop out of the closet. I'd point at a wall and pretend to notice something outrageously funny, slapping my knees, releasing an explosive, riotous laugh. Or I was Groucho Marx, one arm folded behind my back, a hand flicking an imaginary cigar, pacing back and forth in wide strides. When I felt particularly bold, I'd get on my hands and knees to sniff the corner of her prayer spread, scrunching my nose, quizzical. Usually, her fuzzy eyebrows were the first to break, arching severely above her darting eyes. The rest of her face would follow. She'd drop the solemn act for a wondrous mess of glares and grimaces, even as she maintained her Qur'anic recitation.

Invariably, I'd push too far and Bubbi would come unglued.

"My pappy's pappy be damned!" she'd shout. "Bury me a thousand times. Bury me with dung. *That's* what I got comin'. Where's two blinks' peace to say, God O, here, look, I'm not a sinner. I'm not the one shittin' all over heaven and hell. Vile mongrels have it better in this house."

On the rare occasion when Bubbi parented me, she moralized based on her God-fearing upbringing.

"God strikes the sinners," she warned me. "Turns 'em into dust. Blows 'em in the wind. Scattered all over the land, never one no more. It's not right doin' whatever you damn well please, is it? God's a witness to everything. He sees it all."

"Where is God?" I once asked.

"God? *God?*" Bubbi said, like I had turned on her just as she was reaching out to me. God would strike us both, turn us both to dust. And it was never because of anything she had done. Bubbi's way of ending the conversation and mollifying a watchful God was to recite the opening line of the Qur'an: "In the name of Allah, compassionate and merciful."

Of all the incongruities of my youth, God presented the greatest challenge. Here was a being "compassionate and merciful" but also wrathful and punitive. The thought of a kind but trigger-happy God was unsettling. Why would he choose to scrutinize *me*? How did he keep an eye on me? Maybe he could track everyone like radar on the base, scanning the sky until a blip on his screen registered "kid with a foul mouth." My father, given his intimate knowledge of radar, was surprisingly unhelpful in describing God's surveillance methods.

"Where is God? I mean, can he see us now?" I asked him.

"Are you concerned about God or about being watched?"

"I just want to know where he is."

"Take two parallel lines—you can think of them as railroad tracks if you like—and point them up. Let them shoot through the sky and into space. Past the moon. Past the planets. Past the stars. You'll find the answer to your question where the tracks cross."

"Has anyone ever tried that?"

"Not per se. The tallest thing anyone has ever made is the Empire State Building in New York, which is almost four hundred forty-four meters tall. It's actually four hundred forty-three. Don't you think it would have been nicer if they stuck a skewer or something on top so it could be a nice, round number? Four hundred forty-*three* sounds so unfinished. Don't you think?"

At some point in my people's past, my questions would have had unequivocal answers. But so many of our ingrained sensibilities were being rethought to fit the times that when some cultural reflcx actually surfaced, we were left stunned. Once in a while Bubbi would burst in from the kitchen with a tiny pot she'd filled with rue seeds and set on fire. The smoking vessel she rushed around the house was to drive out evil spirits. We sat still as she circled the pot over everyone's head and read her incantations. It was beyond reason to ask, What evil spirits? Why now? Why rue?

We were gripped by an identity crisis, and there was no better symbol of the raging tension than the ongoing comedy of surnames. A product of a government campaign, last names were assigned to households when the first census was taken in the 1930s. For no particular reason, my father's family had been issued Zardeshti, a variant of Zoroastrian, a name they kept for twenty years until Baba convinced his family members to adopt Minu-Sepehr, "Pinnacle of the Heavens," instead. But since reputation was everything, most had kept their government names despite the damage: Protector of Windmill, Lion Tamer, Donkey-Saddle Person.

In the wave of soldiers who came through our house, a corporal by the name of Tootoonchi served briefly as our chauffeur. Tootoonchi meant Tobacco Tender or Tobacco Seller and, as surnames went, was neutral. The staff detested the corporal, who drove our Rambler like it was his own. Whereas other drivers were handsomely rewarded for linking the crew to the outside world of the base, Tootoonchi had no interest in doing anyone any favors and no need for the marrow-filled lamb bones, pickled vegetables, pastry, and fresh herbs Bubbi set aside for him. Corporal Tootoonchi was married and always eager to get the job done as efficiently as possible and return home. Tootoonchi, "deathbed thin," they called him when he left. Tootoonchi, "stiff like he's taken wood up the arse."

When I was five or six and toothless, T was a hard sound to make. I swapped *tootoon* [tobacco] for *doodool* [penis] and called Tootoonchi "Doodoolchi"—or Penis Tender. Mammad egged me on. "That's right," he said. "Good boy. Just like that." Bubbi, reduced to smoking whatever the soldiers managed to smuggle onto the base—"manure brand," she called them—gave her tacit approval by minding her own business.

The first time I called the corporal "Penis Tender" in front of my mother, she quickly brushed it aside. But later, when we were alone, she introduced me to the concept of social spaces—invisible corridors laden with rules.

"You wouldn't come out in front of your baba and say, Oh, look, the dog pooed on the rug," she said. "You would be more discreet. You'd quietly inform Bubbi that Poodie had had an *accident*."

Actually, Bubbi would be the last person to involve if Poodie shat on the carpet; she abhorred dogs and habitually gave her a kick in the butt to be clear about her position.

"Just like you would say some things in front of some people but not in front of others, you can't call Mr. Tootoonchi Mr. *Doodoolchi*

70

in public," my mother concluded. I gathered there was a space in which Mr. Tootoonchi could still exist as Penis Tender.

My hunch was accurate. We cleaved the man in half.

Delineating the licit from the illicit wasn't a simple matter of proscribing certain words. After all, under the tutelage of one foul-mouthed relative, I had turned *ashpaz-khaneh* [soup cookery, meaning "kitchen"] into *shashpaz-khaneh* [piss cookery]; altering one letter in *mehmoon* turned houseguests into monkeys or *mey-moon*; and women of a certain look and flair were, endearingly, whores (this in a culture pathologically protective of its women).

What my mother had to instill in me was a sense of *situational* propriety. What could be said in front of her and Aunt Z, for instance, was different if my father walked into the room. Guests required special considerations. I could be liberal in front of my so-called aunties and uncles, but in the presence of uniformed guests I had to show restraint. (My parents lost one friendship because I called an officer's cleavage-showing wife a *jendeh*. It didn't matter that I had actually called the woman *auntie* whore out of respect.) Strangers, elders, officers, Mr. Tootoonchi, servants, and kids of varying ages demanded different constraints.

It was too much. The contingencies seemed arbitrary. Finally, my mother imposed categorical restrictions. "From now on," she declared, "you are not to say *dool, koon, mameh, kos, folan, tokhm*, or *jendeh* [penis, ass, boobs, pussy, dong, nuts, or whore]."

"Why?" I said. It was as though she suddenly had decided to ban the word *Popsicle*.

The question caught her by surprise. She thought about it.

Because it's wrong no longer held force.

5

A Grand Comedy

By the 1970s we were living in the most intense period of Westernization Iran had ever experienced, when each embrace of the new, each chic turn, posed an affront to a culture already vexed by change. In the very near past, dogs were considered eternally filthy; one lick required seven hand-washings. Pigs were vile; shrimp were vultures of the sea; drinking alcohol was a mortal sin; and women were subject to stern sanctions regarding the visibility of their hair and skin. But as far as I was concerned, dogs were our cohabitants, ham was synonymous with lunch meat, large shrimp were served with white wine, and women wore their hair long and their shorts short.

Some people hid their indulgences behind tall walls and taller conifers, safe, they thought, from scrutiny, with their tight-lipped servants who were expected to see, hear, and say nothing. But, of course, the servants weren't as blind, deaf, or mute as imagined. To Bubbi and her comrades, edicts originating in Paris, Rome, or New York were patently errant—unclean, unchaste, and ungodly. I often found Bubbi grimacing in disgust when she had to wash stemware. Rolling ham slices for a party was particularly offensive to her. Dusting was made more challenging when it meant cleaning the glass sculpture of a naked woman, one arm dangling over her featureless head, a forbidden nymph quietly raising a storm.

In my mother's Darwinian view, there was no social crisis: History was a steady stream of changes that required you to adapt or be left behind. We were fit, she would say; anyone clinging to the past was not. In this view, to be "traditional," to live by staid, outdated practices, was to *opt* to be stupid and inept.

In my father's estimation, the nation's core values were intact, and everything else was a fad.

Aunt Z made a career out of poking fun at the disconnect. She saw rampant hypocrisy. Patriarchy, propriety, the private role of women—undermined by the same crowd whose men preached from their high pulpits, who claimed nobility, and whose women still hid behind their inviolable gender sanctity. The government, too, had blind spots. It prided itself in extending voting rights to women before Switzerland, but it still required a woman's "guardian" to give permission before she could leave the country. The irony of the minister of education needing her father's, husband's, or uncle's consent before she could attend an international summit somehow went unnoticed.

My mother and her sister were negatives of each other. My mother was fair and blond, "like a European," some said, "a Sears catalog girl." Aunt Z had thick auburn hair, an olive tone, and a lush, dark, homegrown beauty. As "Mrs. General," my mother toed a rigid social line, made hierarchy her guiding light, and was quickly riled by any perceived violation of her rightful place. For Aunt Z, an inveterate jokester, one's station in life was an unfortunate barrier to real human contact. She wasn't above cleaning or cooking or mucking it up with the servants.

Their choice in husbands could not have been any different either. Baba was vigorous and athletic, earnest, content, and plain. He was known for his unshakable calm and famously bad jokes. Only once had he gotten drunk. My brother remembered it well:

Baba had spent the night lecturing a dog, admonishing it for barking at a colonel.

"Have you ever said anything bad?" I once asked Baba.

"You mean inappropriate?" he said.

"No, like cursing," I said.

"Cursing for the sake of cursing?"

"I guess."

"Well, what I was getting at is that sometimes it might be appropriate to return a slight with a slight, as when—"

My mother cut him off. "Don't listen to him. As long as I've known your father, he's never cursed. Nothing. He's not capable of it. Not even *poop*," she said.

Uncle P, on the other hand, made foul language his craft. His obscene jokes were legendary. His enounters with the bottle, earthshattering. He was pudgy, had boyish curls, and was never to be taken at face value.

If my mother and Baba were June and Ward Cleaver, then Aunt Z and Uncle P were Bonnie and Clyde. Together, they shot through anything that could be called acceptable, then posed nearby with their smoking guns. At one of my mother's dinner parties for the top officials of Isfahan—suits and poofy dresses, whiskey on ice, and women with big hair—Aunt Z pulled me aside, her eyes full of mischief. I was to deliver a riddle to the governor.

"I'll give the introductions, and you march in," she said. "Stand right in the middle of the salon so they can all hear you. Pull yourself together, no giggles or silliness; you're the general's son! You're making a serious announcement. How would your baba talk to the troops? Like that."

On Aunt Z's cue I walked in, faced the governor, and began instructing the man to say, "One'n one chubby ones I have, one'n two chubby ones I have," and so on till he reached ten.

The entire party and the governor chuckled at the nonsense. "What is the riddle, my son? This sounds more like a tongue twister," said the governor.

"You have to try to make it to ten," I said.

"I see. Something will happen that will keep me from getting to ten, and I have to find a way around it. Very well," said the man earnestly. You could tell he approached any problem this way, rationally cautious but willing. *"Yek-o-yek topoli daram,"* he said harmlessly, eyes darting back and forth in the hush. Then, *"Yek-o-do topoli daram."*

So far, the humor was in hearing drivel from such an esteemed figure, and no doubt the governor was benefiting from the levity. He could mingle with kids and kings alike.

On his third try, *"Yek-o-se topoli daram,"* there was an explosion of laughter. In Farsi, the third iteration with the contracted "and" turns out to mean, I have a fat cunt.

The governor blushed, laughed quietly to himself, and Aunt Z was quick to take credit for the attack. "I'm very disappointed in you," she said to me risibly. "Making a mockery of this establishment."

"The youth these days, Governor!" added Uncle P.

Aunt Z spared no one—the more prudish, the better. At some function where she was seated next to a celebrated economics professor, she asked in all seriousness how someone of his stature and eloquence propositioned his wife. "Professor, I'm curious, do you say, *Darling, kindly draw your buttocks near?*" Noticing the look of horror on the man's face she pointed at Uncle P and said, "My husband grunts, *Hand the muff over.*" She followed this with a graphic description of the sex in *The Last Tango in Paris* and how after the film Uncle P had rushed to a convenience store for a stick of butter. There were reports that the professor spent the rest of the night drinking and dancing, a transformation that propelled Aunt Z to assume leadership of my mother's most dissolute friends.

A Grand Comedy

Often, two men named Cyrus attended our summer socials. They were distinguished from each other as Cyrus the Cousin and Cyrus the Dolphin. To the servants, who were compelled to show respect, they were Cyrus Khan the Cousin and Cyrus Khan the Dolphin. Cyrus the Cousin was an imposing figure. He was tall, dark, had a broad chest of curly black hair, and sported an angular beard that accentuated his square jaw. The Dolphin stood on the other end of the scale, barely making five feet, blind without his thick-framed glasses, flabby, pale, and hairless on face and chest.

One afternoon, while Baba kept an eye on the Soviets, Aunt Z devised a plan to denude the Dolphin at a pool party—he had not yet acquired his nickname. She asked me to get my Hula-Hoop. Each member of the party was made to leap through it as they bounced off the diving board and into the swimming pool. Cyrus the Cousin, half of whose robust physique stuck out of the shallow end, was a natural choice for circus master. He was also the secret agent entrusted with the sensitive trunk-removal. By the time Dolphin-to-be was ready to jump, everyone had gathered around the pool. The diving board arced under its heavy load, heaving the smooth-skinned target into the air, through the hoop, past the deft hands of the Cousin, and out he came, naked. Amid the chaos of laughter and screams, a nude Cyrus emerged floating on top of the water with his member tucked out of sight, making Flipper noises, and shouting, "Come and get it." When the women taunted him, "There's nothing to get," he climbed out of the pool and tore after them, around the rose garden, and up and down the lawn.

Aunt Z had a few, paradoxically deep religious beliefs, which precluded horseplay on Ashura—the one week out of the year during which the nation became righteous. The Shi'a commemoration of Ashura descended like a mood, inflamed the faithful, and gave pause to everyone else.

By second grade, the event had begun to confuse and astound me.

"Me and Mr. K saw a whole bunch of people on the street beating themselves with these things that looked like feather dusters, but the feathers weren't feathers—they were chains!" I told my mother one day. "They swung the chains over their shoulders, and their shirts were all torn up and bloody. But they wouldn't stop!"

"Yup, it's that time when the nuts come out," she said.

"Nuts like crazy?"

"Crazy, faithful, passionate—no difference, my love."

"Cuckoos like from the crazy-people hospital?" You couldn't willfully inflict that kind of pain onto your back unless you had lost your mind.

"Cuckoos, yes, but from a different hospital," she said.

Ashura brought out the zealots, all right. It changed TV programming. It charged everyone with almsgiving—even my mother bought a hundred meal tickets from a local kebab place and had the driver pass them out to the poor. The week occasioned a certain yellow rice-pudding desert, decorated in cinnamon with phrases like "Ya Hussein" and "Ya Ali." God forbid if your birthday landed on Ashura; on this, the most significant Shi'a commemoration, there was no room for anyone except Imam Hussein. And no one could tell me why. My mother's comments were loaded. My father was typically arcane when speaking of religion. And my brother was deeply engrossed in the colonel's daughter. Bubbi's dissatisfying, pat answers offered me nothing. Mr. K who took me to school was my best bet.

"Why are those people beating themselves, Mr. K?" I asked one day over raucous Bandari music.

"They're suffering with Imam Hussein."

"Who's Imam Hussein?"

"Imam Ali's son. Who else?"

"What's wrong with him? Is he sick or something?"

"No, he's dead. They're all dead, all twelve imams. Well, actually, the twelfth one, the Imam of the Age, never died. He's gone into hiding. They say he'll reappear on judgment day."

"Is it judgment day today?"

"No."

"Then why are they beating themselves?"

"Well, when Imam Ali was slain, his son, Imam Hussein, set off with his followers to lead Islam. But when they reached Karbala, a huge army surrounded them and told them to go back. Imam Hussein said get lost—he wasn't going to turn the religion over to a band of murderers."

"Did the big army have a general? What did they say when Imam Hussein told them to get lost?"

"No, I don't know who said what, but the murderers cut 'em off from everything—food, provisions, everything. When one of Imam Hussein's men went to fetch water for the women and children, they sent him back with his hands chopped off. But Imam Hussein didn't give up. He and his men fought to their last breath."

Though it still wasn't clear to me why you would destroy your back to pay tribute to an army defeated by a larger one, I understood that one imam had been outnumbered, and one was expected to reappear. That was Shi'a in a nutshell.

I found the idea of a hidden twelfth imam fascinating. I wondered where he had been hiding, these thousand years, and if there were people actively seeking him. Would he, as in our playground games of hide-and-seek, run back on judgment day and touch the pole or tree designated as base and call out *"sok sok"* to say he was safe?

As it turned out, in the middle of nineteenth century, the twelfth imam—so he called himself—*had* returned. This was the foundation of the Baha'i faith, whose members were brutally persecuted

79

and largely driven from Iran. The twelfth imam was arrested and killed. Maybe he had returned too soon, for the clergy had fashioned elaborate schemes to preside over society in his absence. It wasn't until the 1920s that the clergy really felt attacked. With one wave of his imperial wand, Reza Shah sidestepped the dilemma over the clergy's interim role. He installed civil judges in place of clerical jurists; secular teachers supplanted "schoolhouse" mullahs; state tax usurped tithe; social work ate into religious benefaction. As for the long-standing practice of *estekhareh*—seeking clerical readings of divine signs—it was relegated to hocus-pocus sorcery.

I was spending one Ashura at Aunt Z's house in Isfahan when a mullah in turban and beard, cloaked and in slippers, was welcomed into the house and into the basement. Who had invited him? I wondered. A dozen or twenty of Aunt Z's lady friends in black head-to-toe chadors squatted on the basement floor, waiting. They resembled little tepees. The mullah took the only chair at the head of the room, and after a primer in Arabic—presumably a prayer, but he could just as well have been reporting the weather in Kuwait—he began to describe Imam Hussein and his ill-fated battle at Karbala.

On the main floor, above, *Sesame Street* was on TV. I followed the program with my cousins but was aware of the goings-on in the basement, the spikes in the mullah's narration, and the wailing of the women. The occasional silence was even more intriguing. Had someone passed out? Were they breaking for tea? But then, as though on cue, the ladies burst out in unison, "Hussein, my life, Hussein!"

Mullahs had always piqued my curiosity—no one else walked around with an enormous beard and a funny, honeycomb-shaped hat. Did they have to wrap them every morning? And how did they stay on? I had met a broad cross section of our society through the laborers provided to us by the air force, yet I'd never had an opportunity to meet the most enduring type of man in our nation. And here was one, a real mullah in my aunt's basement, a presence capable of bringing a room full of women to ecstasy. I had to get a better view.

Between the wailing and Big Bird, I snuck down the dank stairwell, blinded by darkness, struck by the volume of the sobbing. As my eyes adjusted, I saw my aunt and her friends quivering and convulsing in waves—such inner Shi'a anguish! Who knew! They shed tears so eagerly that before the mullah could mutter three words, their gales cut him off: "And upon—" "And upon his—" "And upon his dazzling—" "Upon his dazzling steed—" A pack of Aunt Z's friends, huddled together in one corner, were particularly expressive, practically screaming. When I studied them more closely, I found they were hysterically *laughing,* pranking the event with fake wails, mocking the most defining Shi'a ritual under the safety of their chadors.

Maybe they laughed at the anachronism: A mullah had become a comedy skit, his shtick a reenactment of a world we couldn't fathom occupying anymore. Some treaded more nervously around the gulf, feared the gaping historical rift.

In the 1950s, during Baba's flight training in America, my mother had lived in Montgomery, Alabama. Back then, she had found the simmering tensions of a color-divided America incomprehensible. She shook her head when neighbors objected to her black masseuse visiting their white neighborhood. But in her own land, she made a point of keeping to her own kind. She distrusted cross-class interactions. My mother had banned the quickest route to Isfahan, to the city where Aunt Z and Uncle P lived. The road cut through a countryside marked by rough, jagged plots of land, sagging mud huts, and swarthy, leather-skinned men traveling on foot, always with a shovel, pick, or ax cantilevered off one shoulder. The path's many twists and humps made my mother carsick, but she also frowned on the population that inhabited the area— exactly the crowd she thought maladaptive.

In her absence, Mr. K took a deliberate hard left at the beet sugar factory and raced toward the countryside. I loved the roller-coaster effect of the road, and even more, the putrid odor of dung and decay, or fertile earth when it was churned up and damp. Alternately, air pockets of onion and coriander would engulf us, drowning out all other smells. Once, just as Mr. K and I crested a hump in the road, puffs of white started flying over the hood, rolling over the windshield as though we were parting cumulus clouds. Mr. K had no time to react; we delved straight into a herd of sheep and grated to a stop. There was carnage outside and a shepherd running to us, screaming bloody murder, flailing his arms. Mr. K busied himself assessing the mess, shaking his head, looking under the car, popping the hood. Tufts of wool and fragments of skull and brain were jammed into the broken grille. The nasty streak of guts on the road was left by the few sheep we'd dragged along, ground down to the bone. A bunch were on their sides with their legs dangling like string puppets in the bottom of a toy chest. I was too nauseated to register the shepherd's haggling, but Mr. K pulled a fold of bills, stuffed the man's pocket, and rushed to leave the scene. "Get in, quick," he said to me. "The whole damn village will show up in a second."

In the car again, speeding along with the clean whoosh of wind and steady whine of tires already erasing the scene of blood and gore. Mr. K was visibly shaken, dead quiet. I wondered if he noticed the tiny specks of blood covering the windshield or the wisps of wool caught on the wiper blades, tugging in the violent flow of air. The cabin was taking on a peculiar purulent smell, but unlike other passing scents, it was getting stronger. When I made the connection that it was flesh I was smelling, I started gasping for air. Just then Mr. K lifted the smothering silence. "Nothing happened, all right? You didn't see anything. If anyone says, What happened to the car? What was that stuff on the front? Just say,

I don't know. The general won't understand it. Next thing you know I'll have been supposed to make the guy pay *me*."

Mr. K couldn't have been more right; my father didn't understand.

It was only a few weeks later that we drove to a dammed lake, a few hours from Isfahan, where we water-skied in what my father considered competition-quality conditions. On our return, our caravan of three or four cars swerved off the paved road just over a hill to avoid a herd of sheep being led across two lanes. The sun had already set. I was in the first car, in the backseat, and Baba was driving as we bottomed into a rut, sinking deep into the bench seats of our Chevy Impala before pointing skyward, airborne in four thousand pounds of imported steel. We dropped out of the air with a monumental crash and began to spin and skid and slosh to a stop. My mother's scream continued well after our halt, restraining me from saying, Can we do that again? The common sentiment was that we had nearly lost our lives to a bunch of idiots who had decided to roam across the road on the backside of a hill.

Baba left the car and rushed into the plume of dust we had raised, toward the furious shepherd caught in the thin beam of our headlight. The man was beside himself, seething as though we'd violated his most basic right. Customarily, this conflict would take the form of massive posturing on both sides. It would escalate with outrageous threats, puffed-out chests, and fizzle with simultaneous offerings of clemency—*Go on, get lost, you're lucky I'm not in the mood to bash in your teeth*. But Baba wasn't the posturing kind. He grabbed the shepherd by his shirt and in one swift draw of his fist struck the man in the head, knocking him to the ground. The headlights brought a pack of others into view, ghosts materializing out of the dust, dashing toward the entangled pair, wielding their angry staffs overhead. They had funny, camel-like gaits, loping as they ran, lumpy and loose. These people were as much a part of this land as the brush under their slippered feet. Did they even recognize there was a road here? So what that some people came by with big machinery and laid down a black track? Should that have changed anything they did? And what did they think we were doing out at the end of the track? Hanging on to a rope on a couple of planks behind a wedge-shaped thing that cut the water and sped away? Was the wedge trying to get away from us? Did we really think we could catch it?

One of the women in our car spoke up, "Abdi thinks we're still on the base. They're going to kill him." Apparently all the men in our party had the same thought, rushing to intervene before it was too late. Some pried my father back; others calmed the shepherd; and Mr. K negotiated a truce. The general was persuaded to get back into the car, and we pulled out, bouncing toward the road, past twisted faces, swinging canes, and flying rocks.

Had I been observant, I would have taken certain signs in my childhood as proof of coming woes. I often think now about how I would have acted, what I possibly could have said to my father, if I foresaw the horror that awaited us. And I keep going back to the slalom run and the spilled blood.

For a small and tightly knit group of air force elites, particularly those who had belonged to the original Golden Crown aerobatic team, competitive waterskiing was the pastime of choice. So dedicated was this group to the sport that in early years families were packed into single-prop planes and flown to a dammed lake, where, upon landing on the side of a sage-speckled hill, all but the pilot prayed for their lives. Our desert oasis was thus more than a product of human potential; it was an outgrowth of the daredevil and logic-defying spirit shared by the exclusive members of this posse.

A Grand Comedy

In Baba, one of the early leaders of the Golden Crowns, this spirit was amplified. He had installed a slalom course on our man-made lake on the base, and he insisted on besting his own ten-year-old record. I frequently went for a ride as the required observer and watched my father lean almost parallel to the water and carve beautiful arcs around stationary buoys, producing a curtain of spray too tall to make sense.

One summer afternoon, nearing the end of a beautifully clear day, we headed out to take on that formidable record. Baba felt confident. The water was the calmest it had been all day, reflecting every speck of sunset that struck its surface. With my father a rope's length away, we sped to forty knots past the two red orbs marking the entrance to the course. In his second turn, Baba tumbled and twirled and disappeared in the water. His loose line kicked like a rambunctious colt that had bucked its rider and now heaved its haunches in glorious victory. We slowed, reined in the line, and drove back to find, floating upon the shattered surface, broken remnants of the sun and the sky and the man whom I had considered invulnerable, coughing blood. The driver and I pulled Baba into the boat, I unbuckled his life vest, and he groaned heavily with the sway of the boat. Seeing him in this condition back at the dock, my mother panicked. "Don't move him," she screamed. "I'll have him airlifted to Tehran from right here." Baba didn't recognize medical emergencies. You were either dying or engaged in histrionics. He got to his feet, ambled to his Bronco, and drove away. At home, he finally relented to my mother's barrage of threats—I'll call R if you don't cooperate; he'll give the command to G; you'll be banned from flying—and agreed at least to be driven to the hospital in the city.

As a seer, I would have interpreted the setting sun and broken ribs as an unmistakable omen. In the boat, I would have taken my father's head, which lay in my lap, and whispered in his ear. "Meld into the background," I'd say. "Whatever demon you're chasing will be exorcised, and your brand of courage will stand as a national disease. They'll say there was only one way to deal with people like you: death." I would recount as many names of the dead as I could till he was convinced.

6

The Writing on the Wall

A year before the revolution, clashes between government forces and seminary students in Qom made front-page news, but few were troubled by it. The clerical faction's resentment of modernity came in swells. When we visited Uncle P and Aunt Z, dinners ran long. Half a bottle of vodka stood on the dining table, and Uncle P reached for it often. By then, by the time I was nine, there was something noticeably different about him: His ribaldry no longer served an affect; it underscored the seriousness of his position. He was pleading with my father to take immediate action to leave the country.

"It's all going to pot. Can't you see? We're this far shy of being royally fucked—with a commendation letter from the imperial court!" he blared.

Baba tried to reason with him. "Alarmists run and hide. Alarmists pack up anytime someone says boo. We've no reason to get that excited."

"Whatta they gotta do, stick it this far in us for us to say, Well, let's see here, should this excite or worry me?"

"P, dear, what assault? What are you talking about? Where's this bogeyman, this snore-snore-loo-loo?"

"For cryin' out loud. Read anything. They've shittied it all up.

Read Twain, for God's sake. A confederacy of dunces—the lot of them. The writing's on the wall!"

"You mustn't trust all you read. And what do you suppose will happen to the few thousand Americans? And that's just here in Isfahan! Are they all packing their bags? Wouldn't it be funny if we felt less safe in our own land than foreigners? We're no small investment for America, and I have to believe that their capital is safe, that that's why they're not flinching."

"*America?* My dear, America has its head so far up its ass, it couldn't tell you if it were day or night."

As it turned out, the writing *was* on the wall. Literally. Before any hint of death and destruction, the brick wall facing the American school was defaced with big, black letters: "Yankee Go Home." It was confusing. Was there only one Yankee they hoped to expel? Was the lettering made to resemble a second grader's or was it *by* a second grader? Did this represent the sentiment on the street—did all of Isfahan want Yankee gone? More confusing still was that the Yankees didn't seem bothered by it. America was as secure as ever. This, in turn, was supposed to reassure us we were safe.

But even I felt that America was out of touch.

The mainstay of the Persian culture was a hidden language: the precise order in which people entered and left a room; an insistence on elaborate greetings and goodbyes; a feigning of deference and even greater counterdeference. To be cultured meant obfuscating real motives, wrapping intent in pleasantries. The niceties often created confusion or hostility; they left people obsessing over the reasons behind the reasons; they even pitted family members against each other over snowballing misapprehensions. But the alternative, an open book that spelled out every need, desire, and feeling, was deemed, by traditionalists, uncivilized and crude. By contrast, America had introduced frankness into our society, an openness that was the undoing of all things cryptic and Persian.

Without a doubt, Yankee Doodle found Persian ways insufferable. How blissful it was to be ignorant of the strategizing that went into the most mundane activity. Buying grilled corn from a street vendor:

"Thank you. How much do I owe you?"

"*Befarmaeed*. It's not worthy of you."

"Please, how much?"

"For your youngest. You'd make me happy."

"You're too kind. What do I owe?"

"Well, taste it first. You might find you don't even like it."

Being out-charitied by a street peddler drove the average customer into buying a half-dozen more ears and stuffing a large bundle of small bills in the man's shirt pocket. Was this civilized? But when Yankee Doodle shrugged and took the corn, it was as though he had dropped the man on his face and walked away.

Likewise, American foreign policy was seen as being callous, painfully clear with words like *containment* and *détente*. Nixon-era formulations laid out America's approach in no uncertain terms: The United States would reduce its troops abroad and, instead, empower its sympathizers. There was no better example of the resulting "proxy state" than Iran, hoarding American arms to fight an American cause. When the United States pushed for capitulation—that contentious bill that would render all American employees and their families immune to the Iranian judicial system—it was openly trying to protect its citizens. When the Iranian parliament ratified the bill, it openly revealed that Iran's legal system had double standards—good enough for Iranians but substandard for Americans. In and of themselves, double standards were tolerable; but bring them into the open, and they were deemed criminal. According to Uncle P, foreign policy was nothing if not beguiling. "Just look at the British," he'd snort. "How do you think a tiny island rules over half the globe? It slips an arm into someone *else's* sleeve and then smacks whomever it wants."

For the "opposition"—communists, nationalists, and militant clergy against the imperial regime—capitulation was an outrage. Agreeing to suspend our laws for America was tantamount to a loss of sovereignty. The parliament had proven to be a hollow body, rubber-stamping the shah's wishes. And the shah? His fate was sealed as an American puppet. Ayatollah Khomeini, the most outspoken critic of the monarch, decried the acquiescence: If the shah were to run over a dog belonging to an American, he would be prosecuted. But if an American cook ran over the shah . . . no one would have the right to object.

The prevailing position of those who hoped for Iran's membership in the club of developed nations was that we needed to circumvent the long, cobbled path the West had taken to modernity. Who would want to spend years developing the steam engine again when we could appropriate the latest internal combustion engines, hydroelectric generators, jets? The cost no one was willing to talk about was that the jump-start required a compromise.

Having lived through Reza Shah's transformations, my father saw modernity not as a pie in the sky but as a fact of life. To him, it was ungrateful to deride a process through which crystalline drinking water flowed with a quarter turn of a faucet handle. If Baba seemed impatient, it was because Reza Shah's efforts had failed to have a broad and lasting effect on the country. For the architects of modern Iran, those starry-eyed intellectuals who had studied in Europe and America and returned to fashion a nation that would benefit men and women like my parents, disillusionment had set in. To be sure, there was much to be proud of, but also nagging laments. Prime among them was a political process brought to a halt by an autocratic king whose idea of political parties was limited to one—his own. Any lingering talk of democracy was exactly that, empty talk, a thing of theoretical possibility but practical liability. Political activism could land you in Evin, and the regime's use of torture, its human rights violations, was constantly being cited by international watch groups. By the late 1970s, the contagion of optimism so defining of Baba's youth had devolved into cynicism, rancor, and inaction.

But the privileged showed little concern. They were more apt to grease the wheel and let history sort itself out. Fifty years after Reza Shah's program of modernity, progressive and traditional distinctions could have been drawn just as well along age-old divides demarcating the haves from the have-nots. And in this dichotomy, my mother excelled. She knew exactly how the split was maintained. If you asked her, she'd say class disparity never upset the social order; it was Baba—who refused to act the part of a stuffy general—whom my mother blamed as the real problem.

He was defiantly unconcerned with his prescribed role. The man lived by one inflexible mantra—you were who you were because of what you accomplished. If he weren't thinking of a new way to fortify aircraft shelters or honing his flight skills or trying to set a new slalom record, he was fixing something. Our arrival at a relative's house meant my father would first busy himself with a broken vacuum cleaner or radio or a car that wouldn't start. People didn't know what to make of a general on his knees in the bathroom with a dismantled toilet, but Baba wouldn't stop till the thing flushed right.

My mother alternately pleaded with him and threatened him, acting the part of the victim whose life was being ruined by the man whose confirmed tendencies did nothing but "humiliate" her. Were it not for Baba's obstinacy, she was convinced, she would have had *royal* privileges. But Baba was intractable. When all generals were chauffeured, he had his driver take the backseat, and he drove himself. When he and my mother went anywhere, the drivers had the day off.

I looked forward to the occasional luncheons or dinner parties my parents attended. It meant Ab'bas, my mother's driver, would stay home. On holidays, when my brother was visiting, the three of us would drive to the clubhouse and play pool. The clubhouse was in a four-story housing unit converted to a guest quarters for technicians, advisors, and visitors in constant flow. From the outside, the apartment hotel was the same as the dozens of other similar structures, clustered in groups of six or eight, constructed of a khaki-colored brick that extended the color of the desert vertically. One flat was furnished with a pool table, foosball set, lounge, and bar all under dim lights and lowered shades that imparted a fabulously exciting and exclusive feel in a setting that offered no other form of entertainment.

The resident soldier who managed the place was part bartender, part combatant, part servant, part ... magician: When he wrapped his hands around a cue stick the incredible would happen. No frills, no fireworks, no afterburners propelling exotic machines into the clouds, just one ball striking another with uncanny precision, then redirecting itself for the next shot, stopping squarely behind the target as though its path were preordained.

To go to the hotel and hang out with my brother and Ab'bas and the pool divinity was the epitome of cool. Sometimes they rotated me in. Seeing my own clumsy shots made the work of the maestro that much more impressive. I desperately wanted to brag about him, but there was no one to brag to. The rest of the staff had never heard of pool, Bubbi couldn't care less about a ball game, and Mr. K was habitually unimpressed. Mammad, our civilian help, instantly was distracted by the business possibilities. "Does the man there tend a full bar, or is this another kindergarten cafeteria like the officers' club?" he wanted to know. "Is he uptight? Do you think he's a player?" And telling my father meant running the risk of his demystifying the experience. I could just imagine him tracing circles around the bottom of a teacup, explaining the physics of collisions, equal but opposite forces, angles of incidence.

But losing the enchantment of pool to vectors was a concern overshadowed by a more serious danger. There were only a handful of subjects about which my mother was intransigent, and hearing of me in a darkened room with a lowly soldier would certainly pique her worst fears; any hint of such escapades and I'd never set foot in the place again.

One evening, over a volleyball game in the kitchen, Ab'bas touted me a champion for a particularly good shot, lifted me up on his shoulders—"Just watch the hair, boy"—and frolicked up and down the front of the house. "Hooray," he shouted, "Iran takes the gold! Rah, rah." As excited as I was to win gold in the Olympics— it was Ab'bas's highest compliment—I felt nervous on top of the man. My parents had just left, so there wasn't much to worry about; it was just that I'd never done anything that intimate with the help. By the age of nine, I had developed a keen sense of social boundaries and the strictures that governed their separation, but somehow it had all dissolved into a natural, innocent gesture: Ab'bas loved volleyball, I'd managed a superlative strike, and he was overcome with the pride and encouragement of an older brother. And I went with it, wrapping my legs around him, sliding my hands under his jaw. He leapt effortlessly in the air, and every time we landed I could feel the contours of his frame slide against my bare shins, my groin pressing into the back of his neck.

Just then the Impala turned the corner of our driveway like a bad dream and came to a stop in front of us, the width of the driveway apart. Ab'bas and I were ghost struck. We stood motionless looking at my parents, who peered back, equally shocked, through the enormous windshield of the Chevrolet. Ab'bas lowered me with impeccable care as though he had been caught juggling a Ming dynasty vase. He tucked in his shirt and approached the car. Not much was said, some trivial thing forgotten, and I stood where I had been placed, petrified, watching Ab'bas as he ran back and forth to the house.

The staff had followed the encounter with due angst. Was Ab'bas going to get his head delivered to him on a platter?

Back inside, Bubbi thickened the ice. "Death passed the edge of your ear," she said to Ab'bas.

He shrugged it off like he'd done nothing wrong. "The kid's like my own little brother. I can't tiptoe around him like he's a statue."

In short order he was gone.

Months later—with Omid in America, Ab'bas reassigned, and pool a never-again memory—my ears perked up when I overheard my parents speaking of the hotel. A friend of ours was arriving with her two kids and my mother was making a case for them to stay at the hotel. What a gift! I had a legitimate reason to visit the place, and a safe audience with whom I could share pool.

The morning after our friends' arrival, I got up early to take the half-mile shortcut over rough terrain to meet the kids before Mr. K was scheduled to bring them back to the house.

Bubbi wasn't pleased with the decision. "Where you going? What damn hotel?"

"Look." I pointed out the kitchen window to a row of Monopoly-size buildings in the distance. "Over there. They're staying there."

"I don't know about no hotel. Why can't they stay here like normal? So the shitter doesn't work. Have 'em use one of the other ones. Why does anyone need such a big house? A whole village could sack out in the living room. Why don't you wait till K shows up and go with him?"

"No, because the kids are already up and they have nothing to do and Mr. K won't be here for another two hours. This way I can come back with them. It'll be all right. You'll see."

"I don't know," she said woefully. "Anything happen to you and

I'll be hangin' from a tree." The reference to our unfortunate dog wasn't lost on me.

A sliver of desert in front of our house had been tamed into tennis and volleyball courts, but beyond it lay an obstacle course of boulders and ravines and heaps of construction detritus and sun-faded bulldozers and backhoes and augers and trailers whose ceaseless job was to rake the desert into something more habitable. As I climbed my way over this maze, thoughts of billiards quickly shifted to wild dogs. Mongrels were a nagging source of worry on the base, and periodically, to thin their population, Baba called an open season, the carrying crackle of distant rifle fire forming an unnerving backdrop to a life that, in its attempts at establishing civility, had practically removed any sense of danger from our hostile environment. My only encounter with wild dogs had been on my motorcycle, a mile or two from the house, when a pack appeared out of nowhere and began to tear after me. They were the color of the desert, lean, mangy, and fast, and I could barely outrun them at full throttle. Walking across the desert, alone and out of sight, now seemed decidedly stupid. The more I thought of it, the more convinced I became that dogs were stalking me.

By the time I reached the hotel I had broken into a senseless sprint as though vicious dogs were in fact on my heels and reaching the building first would somehow turn them off. Catching my breath, heart still pounding, I glanced back to find the same inert wasteland behind me and no signs of anything alive.

As I had imagined, the kids were up and bored and eager to play. Did they want to see the clubroom just two floors down? "Sure!" they said. They got a groggy approval from their mother, and we were off, chasing down the stairs as though we had a train to catch. I wondered if the custodian I remembered was still stationed at the place, and if he remembered me. The man's peculiar nose, the work of an unjust sculptor giving it pronounced lobes on the sides and a bulbous tip; his light-colored hair, which made him look bald in a military shave; and his quiet, thoughtful eyes were features I had memorized. I used to study him in prominent display under a bank of warm lights cast over the pool table. When the door swung open, I was delighted to find the man's familiar proboscis poking into the light of day. He invited us in and I took pleasure in seeing the nightclub atmosphere unchanged. My friends and I busied ourselves with foosball and checkers and with lounging on the big floppy sofas, and the custodian poured us tall glasses of 7Up adorned with little paper umbrellas. When I asked about pool, the man agreed to get us cue sticks and rack the balls and to show us what to do. A half hour of frustrating shots and worrying remarks from the custodian—my friends were dangerously close to tearing up the felt—and the kids gave up.

"Let's go outside," said the boy, and the sister agreed. To their city sensibilities the desert was much more alluring than a dark room with 7Up and an impossible game.

"You guys go," I said. "I'll come out in just a few minutes." I hadn't risked my life to play in dirt.

The man seemed quietly relieved. He arranged the balls and asked if I wanted to start a "proper" game. I couldn't believe it. The soldier was addressing me like we were old pals. He referred to me with the informal "you"—not as one would the son of a general—and I spoke back to him like a playground buddy. We took turns and made small talk. He asked about my brother and Ab'bas and showed me how to form an arch with my hand and how to hold and drive the cue stick. Pressed close to him, I could feel the man's talent flow through my hands.

I don't know what prompted his sudden request: "C'mon, let me show you something," he said, leaving the room, and I went along. I was one of the guys now and we were doing guy things. When I realized something wasn't right, that I was standing in the soldier's bedroom with no one else around, it was too late. A tightly wrapped bed in a military-gray blanket stared at me ominously. The white walls were closing in. The soldier who had disappeared into his walk-in closet emerged swiftly to lock the door to the room. He slid the key into his trouser pocket and scurried back into his closet without a word. My skin exploded in a rash of sweat as I watched the man undo his belt, his zipper, his pants. He glanced up to look at me, the ridge of his brows casting dark parabolas onto his cheeks, his swollen nose taking on a diseased glow. My heart began to pound. For the first time in my life I felt caught in the tide of something inevitably horrible. I couldn't prepare myself. The tide was ahead of me. Pale thighs. I started to float away.

Then the pounding in my chest spread outward, rattling with the door, shuddering with the room. I was standing in the same spot. Maybe seconds had passed, maybe days. The man was in his closet, naked, fidgeting, but this time in reverse. He was trying to pull his pants up. Thunder. I winced with each strike. "Open this door," came a muffled voice. The door shook violently. Boom, boom, boom; then one monstrous impact as though the door along with its frame were about to come crashing in. The custodian mustered a pathetic "Just a moment please," fishing his belt through the buckle.

"Open it! Now!"

"Coming, coming," stammered the soldier, digging in his pocket for the key.

The man's trembling hand could hardly align the key in its hole. The door went crashing against the wall. My father stood in the doorway. Somebody was going to die.

Baba didn't need much time to assess the situation, the man's shirt sloppily tucked, a child locked in the room. For some strange reason, Baba had a revolver strapped to his hip. He drew it. The man shrieked, dropped to his knees. It was like a film. Gun pointing at his head. My father's square jaw pulsing. I let out a scream and time must have heard me, slowing. When it picked up again, Baba was moving fast. He flipped the pistol around and brought the butt down on the man's back. The custodian was flattened. More blows. Gun hand high up in the air, and down. Up. Down. A few final kicks. The man's wails gave way to muffled grunts. I became aware of my own twisted shape.

Outside, Baba rebuked the kids for abandoning me. He told me to get in the Bronco, and we drove off. Silence. The desert reeling past us at an excruciating pace.

He reached for the handset and got the guard commander on the other end. "Send someone to the hotel apartment to arrest the attendant on duty," he said.

"Yes, General. What should he be charged with?"

"Ask *him* that," said Baba. "Out."

I was dissolving into the big vinyl seat, into the limitless desert, into a cloudless sky.

I didn't know why Baba had come to the hotel. And the terrifying thought, What if he hadn't?

Baba took us over a curb and onto the desert floor. Nothing in sight, my playground turning sinister for the second time in one day. My heart hadn't calmed since we had left, and it quickened once more with the thought that something was about to happen to me again, the way Chubby had left two scars—once when he sank his teeth into my cheek, and once when Baba doled out his punishment.

The miserable diversion came to an end behind a mound of earth. Someone was waiting for us with targets, a clipboard, and a tape measure. It was my father's periodic handgun proficiency test, which was why he had come to get me—we always attended together. Baba took some practice shots with his Colt revolver, fill-ing the desert with blasts that dissipated like dirty little fingers stretching away, polluting the sacred stillness of the air. "Ready," he announced, and the inspector renewed the paper targets. More shots at ten and fifteen. "Put some more up," Baba told the man. My turn.

The gun hung like an anvil from the end of my arm, the sights wobbling in some dream I couldn't shake. An eternity elapsed before the hammer came crashing down of its own volition, snapping the muzzle skyward, fire and smoke. All I could see was the man on his knees, and I was pulling the trigger.

Five more shots. Reload.

No longer could I see the exercise as I once had—accuracy as a sport; focus without reason; a bull's-eye shot devoid of context. Neither was the gun an inert instrument. I was holding an object that had been used to bludgeon a man.

7

Burning Down the House

The next time I saw the gun was one year later, when the revolution had claimed victory and a mounting death toll to show for it.

"What's that for?" I asked in alarm. I was sitting on the edge of my parents' bed, talking to Baba as he got dressed.

He slid a pressed undershirt out from under the revolver and eased the drawer back in. "So that a lifetime's effort doesn't end up underfoot," he said.

I didn't want to know what he meant, but it was clear that the weapon wasn't loaded for paper targets anymore.

The gun made real my central fear that people might come for him. The rest was a given; morgue shots of our friends left no doubt. I had imagined the knock at the door, but it was my father who had seen the scenario through: The rap comes by night, the adults whisper and gesticulate, someone goes to the door, he takes out the gun, aims to kill, blinding flashes of light back and forth, blood. And what am I expected to do? Cower? Scream? Pick up the gun and fire?

To keep my mind off such inevitable scenarios, I had begun to knit. Mamman Ghodsi had shown me a basic knit stitch, and I wasted no time assembling useless sheets of monochromatic yarn.

"Why don't you take a break, my soul, and have some fruit?" she asked me. "Look what Bubbi just brought out. Sour plums!"

"No thanks, I'm almost done with this one."

"Would you like me to show you how to work in another color or circular knit? You could make a winter's cap or some mittens. Thanks to you, we have so many green shawls now."

"No thanks." Shawls required little skill but were full of calming repetition.

"And what lovely shawls they are!" Mamman Ghodsi was never sarcastic. She praised my work heartily and kept a ready supply of green yarn.

When I wasn't knitting I'd stretch out on her plush couch, on my stomach, with my head in her lap, and together we would stare at a wall and ponder the moment. Just as absently, she would drag her soft, ample, manicured hands across my back and scratch my skin in pensive strokes as though she were looking for a way out and my back offered clues. When the inquiry turned into fixed swirls, I'd redirect her, "Mamman Ghodsi, west, west and north, but more west than north," and her obliging fingers would meander over their new coordinates.

The TV offered few escapes. Turning it on, one ran the risk of finding more dire news, more trials ending in death sentences, and righteous clerics promising Islamic justice for the decadent. These weren't fiery sermons aimed to convince and compel; they were cool edicts backed by the authority of God. The one *ancien régime* program the revolution hadn't axed, the one evidently consistent with Islam, was *Little House on the Prairie*—a favorite of Mamman Ghodsi's. Pa and Ma, Laura and Mary and their bucolic problems were just the salve for real lives we couldn't face. What was Nellie Oleson compared to scornful, stubble-faced killers? How sweet the trials of frontier life in relation to a father whose days were numbered. Michael Landon's assured laugh at the end of every episode was a bittersweet reminder of a life we had known all too well, one rapidly turning into a dream. But the *Little House* nostalgia made the show increasingly intolerable to me; it turned our new predicament into a permanent condition of doom and defeat. Halfway through one episode I had a limpid vision of the moment we crested the hill that had put us on this steep slope.

"Mamman Ghodsi, who set Cinema Rex on fire?"

"My dear, Caroline's pregnant, Charles is out there tilling the entire land by himself, and you want to know about Cinema Rex?"

"Yes. Who set it on fire? Why would anyone try to kill all those people?"

"Your questions require divine knowledge, my soul, not me. The beards told us the shah did it; the government said the beards did it. Will Caroline's child be a boy or a girl? Will Charles be able to sow the land before it's too late? Only the Almighty and the cast know. You and I are left to guess."

The torching of Cinema Rex was the most polarizing event in the year leading up to the revolution; it had dominated the news. Four hundred moviegoers smelled smoke. Then the walls were ablaze. Panic. They rushed to the doors but all were blocked from the outside. The lucky ones slipped and got trampled to death before they burned to a crisp.

The TV had covered the catastrophe with horrendous shots of distraught family members picking through charred remains for familiar signs of their loved ones—a ring, shoe, belt buckle, half a face. Rumors circulated that the shah's secret police were the real culprits, that they set the movie house ablaze to frame the clerical faction whose animosity for such symbols of Western culture was well known. The government denied the allegation. It vowed to find the true perpetrators. (Was the concern part of the plan, too?) The clerics decried the senseless deaths. In a televised speech just days before the atrocity, the shah had warned of a great disaster awaiting a nation on a wonton path of revolution. Was this the alluded-to calamity?

I couldn't get over the idea that a theater full of people had burned to death, the popcorn flying, watermelon seeds scattered.

"Did they burn to death?" I asked Mr. K on the way to school.

"Is there some other way to die when you're on fire?" he returned sharply.

"Does it hurt badly?"

"Picture your finger over a candle. Now imagine your whole body over a pit."

No one tried, as they usually did with any news of human tragedy, to convince me that this was an accident or that the crowd had passed on peacefully. There was a national sense of grief, and mourning was the clergy's bread and butter.

Cinema Rex had come on the heels of clashes in Isfahan, the largest city to date to succumb to the rash of antigovernment demonstrations across the country. Crowds, police, and smoke: My daily drive to and from school revealed a national disease. The day Isfahan broke out in flames, rock throwing, and destruction, the governor was visiting us, and my father offered to take him up over the city to gauge the extent of the problem from the air. The next day, General Naji came on the radio to announce a curfew. His soft-spoken way seemed odd, paired with the directive.

And yet my American school continued, unshaken. Fifth grade started with a tour of the new library wing, basketball in physical education, and square dancing in music class. Walking through the school's gated entrance gave me hope there were places left, besides the razor-wire sanctuary of our base, that were immune to the upheavals on the street. Art was still wonderful. In a truly American style, paint came in tubs. Oversize paintbrushes were handed out in coffee cans. And huge sheets of paper—murals compared to the colored-pencil drawings on notebook paper at the Iranian school—were hung for us to paint. Adjoining the library, a fenced-in square of straw-covered earth was the rabbit pen where we could visit the animals during lunch or recess, feed or pet them.

We had started classes at the craft center—one building at the far end of campus in which we learned woodworking, weaving, leather punching, and various other arts and crafts. I took home holiday wreaths, Popsicle skeletons for Halloween, a papier-mâché volcano spewing a lava of baking soda and vinegar. My mother praised my handiwork. Bubbi spurned it.

"What's this?" she said.

"I think a home for bats," I said.

"Bats?"

"I think."

"Great Presence of Ali! Blackbirds, sparrows, filthy feathers stuck to me, shit to shoe. Now I gotta make bat kebabs?"

I spent lunch playing marbles with the other boys who had staked out a dirt-stretch corner of the yard, under a dark canopy of low trees. One marble would be thrown twenty feet out and whoever hit it first would win all other marbles. If you struck someone's marble along the way, you won it outright. The teachers thought of this as gambling, so the game had to be conducted secretively. And the marbles became associative objects of the illegal, the brash. At any one time, safely, you could have five or six in your pocket, and each one had a story. There were lucky ones. Perfectly round ones. Slaves. One boy held his prized possession to the sun to show me a wave of tempestuous ocean blue and a speck of orange. "It's the only one like this," he said firmly. He was a smug kid, disengaged in class, and always busy with something shifty in the yard, his three or four minions ready to follow his lead.

One lunch, I won blue. Everyone was shocked, paralyzed even.

It was almost as though I had ruined their greatest fantasy—blue belonged to the boy leader as the scepter to a king.

Later that day, Miss Lisa called me to her desk.

"Eric says you took his marble. Is that true?" she said in a tone of disbelief.

I was mortified.

A few weeks earlier, my parents had invited Miss Lisa and two of my other teachers to the base, which I took as an assassination attempt on the average kid I'd pretended to be at school for the last three years. My American grade-school setting had been the only place where privilege did not rule, where I'd found it possible to gauge who I was and what I was good at. Now I worried that my sprawling house, my car, the servants and guards, our flower gardens fit for a city park would blow my cover with my teachers. When Mr. K rounded the driveway and came to a stop in front of the house with my teachers in the car, I thought my life was ending.

"Far out, man! So *this* is where you live," said my phys-ed teacher. Mr. Jim was uncharacteristically dressed in a button-up shirt and chinos and had even attempted to tame his mane of hair, which he usually held down with a sweatband. But just as his ensemble made a certain show of respect, he and the others, similarly put together, made a clear statement about their limits: Mr. Jim's shirt wasn't ironed; his hair had only briefly encountered a brush; he wore his default sneakers. Status or no status, America taught you to be comfortable in your own skin.

My teachers wanted to see and ask and converse in the bit of Farsi they had picked up and laugh at their "American" pronunciation of it. I showed them my room—the wall I'd filled with magazine clippings, my collection of Matchbox cars, my *Star Wars* bedspread, my Cookie Monster hand puppet. They were excited to get a ride in my car and to throw a Frisbee around on the lawn, and Mr. Jim amused everyone by riding my motorcycle up and down the driveway, pulling wheelies, and veering off onto the lawn to crash clownishly. Haji, the base chef, was brought in to grill his famous kebabs, and as my parents were drawn into a conversation about the future of Iran around a picturesque circle of lawn furniture aglow in the wild flicker of candles and a tangerine sky, Mammad kept appearing with trays of tea and lemonade and wine. On his return to the kitchen, he stopped by the grill to make sure Haji's vodka was topped off, and he stole two skewers of kebab.

But it wasn't privilege that came to haunt me at the American school. It was pity for a boy whose home was falling apart.

"I'm sure it was a misunderstanding," said Miss Lisa. "Please return his marble and go to your seat."

I wanted to cry. I wished I were being punished like anyone else. But the sum total of everything I was and everything I represented suddenly stood between us like a monument. I could no longer be another kid.

One project at the craft center involved candle making. Our class formed a circle around four or five vats of hot wax, and we took turns dipping the two ends of our long wick into the different colors. Layer after layer, color after color, two conjoined candles grew. It was like watching the hour hand of a clock; you knew something was happening but couldn't track the progression. Waiting in line led to horseplay, pushing, and one of the boys across from us knocked into a vat, which sent it toppling toward me. Hot wax came pouring over, splashing all over the shop floor, and covering my lower half. The class gasped. Our shop teacher rushed to me as though I'd been shot, soaked in blood.

"Are you hurt?" he yelled.

"No," I said.

"Are you sure?" He was still yelling.

"Yes."

The man ran and got some paper towels, knelt by me, and

started wiping my hardening, crusty pant legs. "It'll be all right," he said. "You'll see. It's all going to be all right."

It was then that I fully realized how desperate we had become. In normal circumstances, no teacher would have kowtowed to a student; no man would have offered tremendous assurances when his classroom had been destroyed.

Uncle P's predictions were coming true. He decided to liquidate his life's possessions and move his family to London. Given his track record, no one put it past him to move by himself if anyone resisted.

"What about Z and the kids? You can't just sell the house from right under them and relocate!" My mother was never afraid to speak up when her sister fell silent. She was eager to stress this was not the best time for chauvinistic games.

"If the pussy-giving sister is bent on testing her stupid luck, so be it. As for this shuffling cane-toter, the path has turned too cobbled to continue."

"What cane? A robust forty-year-old pretending to be the weakling. Why not stand up straight and face this like a man?"

"Very well," he said. "Gather ye far and near, I hereby relinquish any and all vestiges of manhood to this maiden so that she may defeat darkness and usher peace and prosperity for all. Amen."

For those who drew lessons from history, revolutionary eruptions echoed earlier, vain struggles against the regime. The 1950s saw masses taking to the streets in defense of the populist prime minister. Demonstrations, shootings, deaths. They had even won: The shah fled the country. But within days those same masses bore witness to a coup (of British design and American implementation) that restored the throne.

Cinema Rex shook the establishment in ways the uprisings

could not. Maybe the shah imagined, as I did, the horror of innocent people sizzling to death. Perhaps the regime realized it had been buttressing the wrong wall, that with another untimely disaster the tide of popular opinion would crumble the power structure. The shah made a conciliatory gesture by replacing his prime minister with an adversary whose quick reprisals against the establishment aimed to appease the conservative faction: Casinos were shut down; the imperial calendar reverted to its Islamic year. It was too little too late, or, as some feared, too much too soon; a concession after Rex was taken as a sign of culpability.

The gambit paid off poorly with a spate of new demonstrations across the land. Just after Cinema Rex, a mass march in the capital city led to an explosive clash with the army. Reports came of tens or hundreds dead—or tens of hundreds, depending on which "freed" media you listened to. Black Friday, as the day came to be known, drew massive criticism from various groups who, until then, had remained neutral. It was possible Palestinian snipers co-opted by the clerics had incited the army into firing; maybe it was even true that red dye was dumped in city gutters to fake a massacre. But an erosion of faith in the instruments of the government, in all public officials, lent credence to the most nefarious conclusions. Western media were abuzz, ecstatic to reveal the dark side of a close U.S. ally whose king President Jimmy Carter had just lauded as having the "respect and admiration and love" of his people. Michel Foucault, the French intellectual superstar, settled in Iran to report on "the perfectly unified collective will" of its people, giddy in defending Islam as the harbinger of the next phase in world political order. Black Friday was a rallying cry. In the aftermath, I overheard a close family friend, the daughter of a millionaire entrepreneur, confide in my mother. "We're walking against the shah this weekend," she whispered.

The most devastating aspect of the revolution was its capacity to attract vastly diverse groups when in fact it had a narrow, intolerant trajectory from the start.

People marched against a common enemy, but it wasn't clear who the enemy was. Who was fighting whom? Driving to school past tanks, troop carriers, and soldiers hiding behind piles of sandbags made a confused, if not menacing, impression on me. With its awkward barrel sticking into the street like a downed light pole, a tank looked oafish in the streaming mélange of mopeds, pedestrians, taxis, and street peddlers. "Fanta, Pepsi, Canada Dry"—a familiar beat-up icebox being pushed on squeaky wheels, the man ducking under the tank's barrel rather than walking all the way around it.

Before the army's presence hinted at a troubled core, Isfahan made a convincing case for the symbiosis of modernity and antiquity. Here was a city that apparently balanced steel mills and minarets "without any sign of strain on its brow." Isfahan was home to the most sophisticated fighter jet in the world and to some of the best examples of Islamic architecture, to vibrant Shi'a theologians as well as to Jews and Armenians and dozens of synagogues and cathedrals. Vank Cathedral, the most famous structure in the Armenian quarter, was a striking marriage of Islamic mosque on the outside and Christian imagery on the inside.

The centerpiece of Isfahan—once Iran's capital—was its four-hundred-year-old city square called Impression of the World. The sixteenth century was no modest time for Iran, with architecture as grandiose as the inflated personalities who wielded power. The square was a massive rectilinear spread with central gardens overlooked by the ancient royal palace, two mosques, and the grand bazaar. Stretching between these poles of Iranian society—monarchy, religion, and commerce—were workshops with graceful, arched entrances leading to artisans bent over their wares, busy striking, polishing, painting, chipping, and weaving in a kind of dignified labor borne out of centuries of learning and mastering and mentoring. With consumerism increasingly shifting value away from craft and toward vapid innovation, Isfahan's lively workshops made an important statement that the two were not mutually exclusive, that we were not facing a historical precipice.

Isfahan was inarguably the site of the most significant development in Iran's recent history. Four hundred years earlier, Shah Ab'bas had made Shi'ism the state religion. The clerical class this turn empowered, the one nurtured by a succession of kings and dynasties and even by the current shah himself, was the one that now aimed to bash the king's head and run off with his scepter. But religion's authoritative claim wasn't as unprecedented as it suddenly appeared. In the course of the twentieth century, the clergy and the merchant, or *bazaari,* class had come together to check and balance the monarchy's often far reach. What was new in the latest test wasn't the activism but the concerted effort by the *bazaari* class to fund a militant branch of clerics who looked to Ayatollah Khomeini. The ayatollah, in turn, sought to put an end to two thousand years of kings. What would follow was anyone's guess.

One look at the artifacts in Isfahan and you would never think of partners colluding to sack the monarch. There was a seamless merging of king, mosque, and bazaar. The Shah Mosque stood as a testament to the old king's commitment to Shi'a Islam. Flying over Isfahan, as my father and I often did, you could spot a dewdrop of turquoise from miles away occupying one side of the Impression of the World. On foot, the tear-shaped top revealed itself as a mesmerizing pattern of aquamarine mosaic tiles laid, one at a time, over the ethereal dome. A circumference of black, intertwined letters spelling out Qur'anic suras were too stylized to decipher but a sign of the moral underpinnings of society, nonetheless.

Mosque domes, which relied completely on their characteristic shape for support, were an exacting engineering feat. Standing in the great hall of the Shah Mosque, it was easy to believe that it was indeed an act of providence that a roof of such precarious height and span could hover overhead. In the minor chamber adjoining the hall, I could stand right under the center of another bowl-shaped ceiling and eavesdrop on private conversations taking place on the periphery or try to count the number of reverberations produced by a single hand clap.

Baba was moved by the physics of mosque domes and always by the learning opportunities at hand. "If this were a smoother dome you could expect a few more claps to echo back. Imagine it more and more exact, and still more claps would bounce back. Now tell me, why can't you expect to hear an infinite number of echoes with a perfect dome?"

"Because we would get tired and go home?"

"Ha! That's one way to look at it, I suppose."

The architectural wonders of Isfahan, however, were no match for the wonder of flirtation, which I was also introduced to on the Impression of the World. Once, I had occasion to spend an entire day at the square with my brother. For him, the outing presented an opportunity to go on an unchaperoned date with a girl he'd been seducing on one of his visits. So as not to appear too easy, the girl had brought four of her cousins, making an impenetrable clique of boisterous, attractive women, seemingly satisfied with their own inside jokes and coded Farsi. Making the best of it, my brother basked in the envy of ogling men. He ambled behind me with his women, and I had a rare chance to sample the city.

"D'you think I could have corn?" I asked him.

He handed me a large bill in front of the ladies and said, "Buy all he's got if you like."

"Can I dunk it in his brine bucket?"

"That's the best part," he exclaimed.

The women grimaced and screamed. "No, don't, it's absolutely disgusting. Oh my God, it's full of spit. You'll get syphilis. Tell him not to."

It was all I could do to control my excitement. Standing in line I rehearsed how I would take a bite and dunk, bite and dunk. Street corn, to say nothing of the community brine bucket, was considered low class by my mother. She encouraged fondue instead.

Sprinting back and forth to our group, I led everyone to a Ferris wheel. It was nothing to get excited about—five or six rickety seats swaying up and down to a proprietor's careless arm turning a hand crank. A knot of squirming kids clambered, yelled, and begged to get on. The thing was a far cry from the hundred-year-old Ferris wheel I'd ridden in Vienna's Prater, the world's tallest when it was built. The Riesenrad was a sight to behold, with cars the size of buses, a football field's ascent, turning with Model T speed—a ride with such politesse, even my mother endorsed it. But the sheer thrill of getting picked for a ride on our own jalopy was unmatched by any record-breaking machine I had been on.

When the riots engulfed Isfahan, Mr. K and I once got caught in a demonstration. A sea of screaming people with raised fists completely drowned the traffic, bringing us to a standstill. The horror of getting moored in a mass protest in a government vehicle took a bizarre turn: They were blaring, "Long live the shah!"

"What's going on?" I asked Mr. K. You could have expected anything but a *pro*-shah demonstration.

"Who the hell knows," he said, frustrated.

That same night there was a tentative sense of relief at Uncle P and Aunt Z's house, a lull spoiled by all the boxes everywhere. Uncle P's moving process was in its final stages; he had found a buyer for the house, and Aunt Z was still in a state of shock. Though she showed considerable restraint, you could tell that my mother was burning to light into Uncle P, to say, You see how ridiculous you've been? People clearly love the shah!

Uncle P interpreted the turn of events as the most troubling development yet. "Some mullah has a dream in which the shah seems okay, and this is the result? What this nation has proved is that it's governed by fart. If it blows in from the east then they'll kill the king. But if it sweeps in from the west, because fart has a chic scent from the west, then they'll love him."

My mother had no ideological drive, but it rankled her that her sister's life was being turned upside down by a man prone to dramatics.

"The trouble with you, my dear, is that you'll twist anything to get what you want. There is no clearer expression than what happened today—the majority rising up against a bunch of thugs who set four car tires on fire and call it a revolution."

Yet, driving home past curfew, through a deserted city choked by roadblocks and soldiers, pushed any idea of restoration out of our minds. This conflict hadn't seen its end. Tomorrow still hung in the balance.

The mourning cycles continued around the country, but in Isfahan there was a semblance of peace and order—and languor on the part of the military. Idle tanks turned into fixtures. Soldiers looked bored. The buzz of army vehicles around the city had all but died down. As though to call the regime's bluff, one day people came out en masse, walked up to the soldiers, and stuffed carnations down the muzzles of their guns. If the military itself wasn't bizarre enough in its urban locale, driving past rows of army-green men with white flowers sprouting out the tips of their guns was surreal.

Making the most of his two measly stripes, Mr. K capitalized on the fact that he outranked the soldiers on the streets and that he had a direct line to the general. A few times, just for fun or because he simply could, he brought us to a screeching halt at the exit gate of the base and ordered one of the guards to get in the car. "The general's son." He pointed at me, as though the rest was self-explanatory. With my helmeted escort propped in the passenger seat squeezing a tall gun between his legs, I arrived at school a half hour early, slipping past all the roadblocks with amazing efficiency. Mr. K never lowered his window for the army men, raising instead a few fingers as though he were of stratospheric rank and it was a petty chore for him to have to acknowledge such lowly underlings.

Despite this measure of ultimate control, he had begun to carry a revolver in a detective holster under his coat. Given his barrel chest and ill-fitting uniform, the gun's handle formed a small tepee on one side of his chest, which prompted total strangers to point or, worse, help smooth out the snag. When I asked him about the gun, Mr. K said, "General's orders," rather pleased with himself.

I took the question right to my father. He explained with a dose of circular reasoning that Mr. K was now my bodyguard and "what good would a bodyguard be if he couldn't guard a body?"

"Why do I need a bodyguard?"

"I wouldn't call it a *need,* per se; it's a precaution."

"What's a precaution?"

"The shin guard you wear when you play soccer is a precaution. Against what? Against someone's foot ending up in your shin. Do we care that the person intended to bury their foot in our shin? No; there's a ref whose job is to worry about such things. Our job is to focus on the game."

"Oh," I said contentedly.

An armed Mr. K was a safeguard against anonymous men calling our house and threatening to abduct me. If the conflict on the street were ever to turn into widespread revolution, it would need to weaken the power structure in ways that went above and beyond annoyance; it would need to break its will. And they couldn't have chosen a better target. Of all the investments my father had made in his country, I was his greatest achievement, raised to see no limits, to imagine a boundless future for Iran.

Whatever Mr. K had been told made him perform his duties with less mirth. He no longer played love songs from his secret tape deck. No more snapping, dancing, or crooning. Instead, he wore a low-grade frown, sign of a running preoccupation that came with his new commission. The man followed my every step: on the edge of a playground; planted on the side of the volleyball court; hovering over me as I tried on a pair of new Adidas. The only respite from my ill-shaped shadow was when I attended school where, with the heightened security, the American turf was thought to be impenetrable. But outside the school's gate, there he was to walk me back to the car in a close escort as though our clothes were made of Velcro that grew more and more entangled with each step.

In autumn the American school announced its closure. A teary Miss Lisa informed us we would finish the rest of fifth grade in America. There was only one person to whom that pronouncement didn't apply, and as soon as she spoke, I felt all eyes land on me. Miss Lisa couldn't hold back her tears. She looked at me apologetically, and a lava of grief welled up in my throat.

There was an America that was a superpower, that could send men to the moon, restore failed monarchs, and make Coca-Cola a household name. And there was an America that wore T-shirts and jeans and its heart on its sleeve. Without a doubt, individual Americans represented the latter, and Iranians played the role of gracious host. When Miss Lisa shed tears, she suggested it was our countries' failed relationship, the goodwill of one people for another caught in the crossfire of grand schemes that was sending my classmates out of my country, leaving me behind.

Soon, the last day of school arrived and I walked around in some sort of daze as though the only way to deal with the disaster was to forestall the feeling. It was only with such emotional distance that I had the fortitude to hug Miss Lisa and to say goodbye to my classmates and to Brooke, the blonde whose steely, confident eyes and tomboy brazenness I'd kept in my thoughts throughout grade school. Secretly, I had dedicated a good number of my drawings of cars or soldiers or airplanes "to Brooke." Mr. Jim's parting words and three-part handshake lightened my mood. "Don't forget the moves I showed you on your bike. Right? Tell the general to keep it loose."

Following Mr. K to the car, I left the American school and all its inhabitants behind me. I peered out from the backseat over a city saddened with soldiers, guns, scrappy little cars speeding past spewing black smoke into the air, and depressed-looking pickups, their beds crammed with dirty sheep. That evening I grappled with Mr. Jim's message for my father. Was it better to convey it verbatim or translate it? Baba, my physical education teacher said that you should maintain slackness? Maybe it was better to try to capture the intended meaning. But what did he mean? I could just hear my mother, You mean to say someone tells you to tell your father such a thing and you receive it like a clueless turnip? Most exemplary! Well done! Next time someone says such filth to you, you say, Tell your *aunt* to hold it loose.

In the end I determined it was more prudent to bury the comment with the turmoil of the day.

"How was school today?" my mother asked over a somber dinner.

"Good. I said goodbye to everyone and they went to America." And that was exactly how it happened; as soon as we said our goodbyes, America pulled out of Iran—nowhere to be found again.

* * *

I began to attend the Iranian school on our base in Isfahan where, given my father's commanding presence, I was a celebrity and equality was the last thing to expect. Privilege was a double-pronged condition: The respect accorded the general's son brought with it higher expectations. I faced a ceaseless internal dialogue. Could I horse around with the other kids? Could I tell a joke? What if I used off-color words? The teachers didn't help matters, enforcing a different standard that seemed to prove to themselves that there really was something special about the son of the base commander. When no one else could answer some question, our teacher would call on me to go to the board and explain. The way she asked me laid bare her assumptions. "Aria dear," she'd start, "why don't you show them how to do it." The phrase "Aria dear" contained a first name *and* an endearing tag while the rest of "them" were sentenced to stern last names.

After school, I spent my free time in the kitchen with Bubbi, dismantling electrical appliances.

Bubbi seemed strangely tolerant of this, but every now and then she cast a reproving look at me and said, "It's only fair that you're his seed."

"Don't worry. I know how to put it back together. Besides, we have another toaster."

I also had become an avid caricaturist, transforming all the mullahs who now filled the newspaper. It was endlessly delightful to change the turban into the bubble helmet of an astronaut, to add a space pack and clumsy boots and set a bearded cleric adrift in space. Or to turn a set of mullahs into cabaret dancers. In that case, I decorated turbans with colorful plumes, made the dancers loop arms, and jutted their fishnet legs out from the curtainlike folds of their tunics.

Occasionally, my eyes fell on a glaring headline: "Shah Orders Arrest of Thirteen Officials." "Prime Minister Taken." "Shah

Admits to Corruption." With no one but Mr. K and Bubbi to turn to, I would try unsuccessfully to hold my questions until dinner.

"Mr. K, what does it mean that 'the shah heard the voice of the revolution'?"

"It means that until he hears it, nothing's happening."

"Did he really arrest Mr. Hoveyda?" Amir-Ab'bas Hoveyda was the longest-running prime minister, iconic for his orchid corsages, cane, and pipe. The man spoke better French than Farsi, was our trump card against the West, and was reviled by traditionalists.

"The days of a man pinning flowers to his chest are over," said Mr. K.

I knew better than to involve Bubbi in politics; she admitted she "didn't know nothin' 'bout no revolution." But she showed increasing bitterness over my artwork. In the middle of one of my cancan alterations, she stomped over to tell me, "These people are holy. You got no right doin' whatever you damn well like." It was the first time she had resorted to "rights" as the basis of anything, and it stood between us as an odd, new, irrevocable development.

Just before Baba left for Tehran to assume his new post, news came that Ayatollah Khomeini would fulfill a Qur'anic prophecy and appear in the moon. The day after, the sighting made headline news. Bubbi was frozen in front of the radio with her head askew and one hand hovering midair holding a spatula.

I could sooner accept the ayatollah had landed on the moon than understand how he could have *appeared* in the moon. Listening as intently as Bubbi to the radio, to men and women gravely moved, I concluded that something bizarre had happened and was curious to know the exact mechanism by which one appears in the moon. Bubbi kept muttering, *"Allah-o-akbar."* God is grand. She turned to me and, as though she had just processed what had happened said, "It's a sign."

"Baba, how did people see Khomeini's face in the moon?" I asked over dinner.

"People can see whatever they want, wherever they want to see it," he said.

"But *was* he in the moon?"

"No, he was in Iraq for twenty years. They just expelled him, and he went to Kuwait, which didn't grant him entry. Now he's in France."

"So what did people see then?"

"They probably likened the shadows on the moon to his face, the way you can pick out shapes in cloudscapes. Your mom's good at it. She'll point at a patch of clouds and say, There, a cocker spaniel chasing a ball. Then you're stuck trying *not* to see a cocker spaniel in the sky."

"Do you think some people in America saw his face too, or could they only see it from Iran?"

"Since most rational people don't believe that faces can appear in rocks, we can safely say that Khomeini was only seen in Iran—and only by those with overactive imaginations."

"What your father means to say is that a bunch of lunatics are running around making up dangerous things, and our people are just crazy enough to believe them," added my mother.

My father would fill his new office at the air force headquarters in Tehran before we could join him, a few months later, in spring. My mother was elated to be moving to the capital. She had longed to rejoin what she called "civilization" and to put behind the itinerant life she had led on one far-flung air base or another. Through it all she had climbed social ladders to the top in any of her parochial settings. Now she was eager to attack the major leagues.

But spring seemed to recede further with the passing of every interminable day. The desert's leveling winter only added to the chill created when my father left. No more dignitaries. No officers reporting at night. Nothing left to inspect, no engineers to hound or projects to monitor. The kitchen, too, was a ghost of its formerly bustling self. All the soldier-servants were sent back to the barracks with the exception of Mammad and Mr. K, who still followed me around—my parents could not rule out the possibility that the ongoing threats against me were coming from within the base. When we closed parts of the house with heavy drapes over the furniture, I had the impression of being buried alive. My mother and I spent the evenings nestled together in the family room, and I anxiously listened to her ideas of what awaited us in Tehran.

"You'll start at a good private school and make great new friends that you'll keep for life. Tehran is so incredibly beautiful, you'll wonder how we've endured in this forgotten place for so long. From one angle of our house you can see all of Damavand to the north, covered in snow, and you and Baba can go skiing every weekend."

"How come I've never seen our house?" I wanted to know.

"Well, my love, it's not quite ready. They're working on it as we speak. I planned for a neoclassical entrance, a half-circle marble landing with fluted columns and capitals shaped like rose bouquets. Open the door and you walk into a grand foyer beyond which a glorious staircase winds up to the bedrooms. I had the architect—"

"Will Bubbi still sleep in my room?"

"She'll have her own room, a bathroom, and a little—"

"But what if she *wants* to sleep in my room?"

"You'll have an armchair in your room, and she can sit next to you as long as you like."

"Will we have a kitchen with people in it?"

"What kind of kitchen has no people in it?"

"I mean a place with soldiers and drivers and Mammad. Will Haji come to cook for us anymore?"

"We'll have staff commensurate with a house of that size, if that's what you're asking. As for Mammad . . . I think I'm stuck with the goon for life."

I was seated in the front row where, in the hierarchy of Iranian schools, the best students benefit from the instructor's doting attention while the ones who really need help are distanced from the board, with the most hopeless cases segregated into oblivion in the very back. We were in the middle of a dictation, and I was trying hard not to misspell, fearing that if anything would prove it was privilege and not talent that had gotten me a front-row seat, it would be the curse of Farsi's redundant sounds—four letters for Z, three for S, two each for T and H. A forceful knock on the classroom door broke my concentration.

"Yes," said the teacher.

The door swung open. Mr. K pushed into the room with his gun in plain view. "Pack your bag," he said to me. "We need to go."

The teacher, an officer's wife, cut in. "What's this about? Is anything the matter?"

Mr. K found it beneath him to answer a woman. "Make it quick. I'll wait outside," he said to me and left.

I made a show of deference and started to collect my things. "With your permission, Missus," I said and raced out.

I couldn't imagine what would have required me to return to our empty house. On the drive home I couldn't get anything out of Mr. K. For him, any exercise of authority, especially if it caused torment, was fabulously enjoyable.

The car had barely come to a stop in front of the kitchen when

I dashed out to pry answers out of Bubbi. "What's going on?" I asked. "What's the matter? Why is Mr. K being so strange?"

Bubbi stood calmly over her stew, stirring it without looking up, clearly not surprised to see me back. "They called and said they're gonna burn the house down."

"Who called? What house?"

"This house. They're gonna set it on fire with me and you and Missus in it."

8

The Escape

It was as though Mr. K had thumbed a book open to its moment
of crisis, picked me up, and dropped me into the pages.

"What are you talking about?" I asked Bubbi.

"What do *I* know? I've only got a burnt tongue for a soup I
never had."

"Where's my mother?"

"Inside, tellin' 'em to kill us. Oh, God, what did I ever do?"

I found my mother on the phone, intent and inexorable. "And
what is the occasion? No, thank you, please tell your wife we won't
be able to come to dinner. And do tell them I said they should proceed with their plans. My son and I prefer to watch the show from
the inside. You're very kind to have called." She slammed down
the phone.

"What's happening?" I asked.

"This is the way they want to thank your father. Four years of
sweat wasted on a forsaken base. Don't go outside till I figure this
out."

It was nothing personal. More had happened in the last few
weeks than in the preceding year. The shah had appointed yet
another prime minister and left the country; Ayatollah Khomeini
had returned to Iran claiming victory. Whose government was
the legitimate one? The military stood as the arbiter. Whomever

the armed forces—specifically the air force, given its lethal, aerial advantage—showed allegiance to would win. Perceptively, the ayatollah focused his rhetoric on air force personnel, and it fueled the first fire. Elite officers loyal to the old order heeded the shah's prime minister while the lower-ranking NCOs looked to Khomeini. In Tehran, in the last day or two, air force NCOs had begun attacking other armed forces and had opened an armory to the public. On our base, home to the most sophisticated operation in the country, the thinking seemed to be that if they razed the commander's house—meaning ours—then the entire operation would fall. Other bases would follow suit. The fight would move to the street, where Khomeini's henchmen thirsted for blood.

In refusing to leave, my mother drove a wedge into the local NCO movement. The militant crowd pushed to burn the house, satisfied they had given us ample warning. Their more "sensible" brethren thought it would be counterproductive to kill the commander's wife and son in the process. Alive, we could be held as bargaining chips in the unfolding drama.

When night fell, a misty rain thickened the air, and an ominous procession of cars filled the only road running by our house. It was an eerie sight, a string of headlights encircling us on a path that was usually empty. Was the whole base out to get us? Was loyalty that fickle? Had there been some sort of advance on the main gate that let in a swarm of revolutionaries?

Gathering in Bubbi's darkened kitchen, we watched the flame of headlights run deep and long on the wet road, threatening at any moment to come torching up the driveway. When my mother had seen enough, she stormed out of the kitchen and went back to the living room. Bubbi peered out over the lights and wrung her hands.

"I knew this was gonna happen. Judgment day is here," she said. "God's come to strike down on us. All my bunk prayers! The damn dogs. Pork. Wine. But who's to say, No, don't kill her, this one never tasted no wine. Mammy, where are you to see your flesh and blood hacked to bits? For naught. What did *I* do? Hacked because I'm damned. Hacked and no one to say, Leave this one. This one's good."

In Bubbi's view, we faced the wrath of God's soldiers. As far as my mother was concerned, we were subject to an insolence she would punish as soon as she identified the naughty kids involved. But this was *my* base: *I* had controlled its traffic violators; *I* had curtailed gabbing soldiers; it was I who imagined being charged with keeping the peace in the general's absence. To wait helplessly, to watch it fizzle out of control was to let Baba down. I sprinted to my room, grabbed my rifle and a box of pellets, and snuck back to the kitchen.

Seeing me load the gun and point it out an opened window sobered Bubbi. "Put that away, ehh! It's not enough to be burned? You want 'em to shoot us, too? In the name of God, merciful and compassionate! Oh, why did I ever leave my home? Mammad, go tell the missus the kid's got a gun. Tell her they're coming to hack us for sure now. Put that away, you hear me?"

I was possessed by a determination that overcame rationality. I followed one car at a time in my sights. This one. This one. That one. And I knew with more certainty than I'd ever felt that I would shoot the first one to head for the house.

My mother came crashing into the kitchen, a gloating Mammad trailing behind her. "What do you think you're doing?" she said to me, more perplexed than upset. "I was certainly not expecting anything so mind-boggling from your father's son. You just wait till I get him on the phone." Then, turning reprovingly to Mr. K, who had just walked in and had no idea what was going on, she said, "Why do we need *you* if we're going to arm the kid? Don't just stand there like a castrated bull. Take that thing from him!"

Mr. K charged me and tore away my gun. "No buts," he said, pushing me back with one outstretched hand. "You heard the missus."

I sulked in the living room, where my mother had resumed her heated phone calls. Thinking of my father, I could only imagine his silent disappointment when he learned of what I had done. And there was no doubt in my mind; she would tell him. Since that afternoon, my mother had been trying to reach air force headquarters by phone, and my stunt renewed her purpose. I could say I wasn't really aiming at anyone in particular but at their vehicles. I could reassure my father I was only prepared to fire aerial shots. I wasn't stupid. Was I stupid? I could list fifty ways I had proven not to be stupid.

Amid these internal deliberations, with my mother on hold, Mr. K came stomping in. "Missus, the gun is loaded and we can't get the pellet out."

My mother turned to me, covered the receiver, and said, "You must be proud of yourself."

"You've got to shoot it to get the bullet out," I told them helpfully.

"Outstanding!" she hissed at me. Pushing her palm deeper into the receiver, she whispered to Mr. K, "I don't want a loaded gun in the house. Take him with you and figure out what to do with it."

Back in the kitchen, to Bubbi's ceaseless narrative of doom and despair, Mr. K and I wrapped the gun in a blanket and slid out in back of the house. A muffled blast emptied the morsel of lead I had figured would block a revolution.

Inside, the television was brimming with news—the arrest of General N, head of the secret police. Sticking out the back window of a sedan, the general's face was bruised, torn, and bleeding. In the looping, few-second clip of the car rolling by the camera, the man bellowed hoarsely, gasped for air, and took hits in the head from the crowd who had gathered to see his arrival. It was inconceivable to me that a *general* could end up like this. Where were his men? What higher authority was there?

A cold sweat covered me: What if we couldn't reach my father because he, too, was being hauled away?

Just then I heard my mother utter Baba's name into the phone. He was safe. We were safe.

". . . So I told them to go ahead and burn it, that we weren't going anywhere," my mother told him. "Now they're circling the house in their cars trying to scare us out. Fat chance. I'm not going to give in to a bunch of opportunists. Who do they think they're dealing with? They've grown tails!" She paused to listen to him. "You don't think they'll actually burn the house, do you?"

There was talk of other things. "What's going on there? The TV's showing awful things. Are you safe? What should we do?" I hoped that my antics would be forgotten in the midst of graver issues, but no such luck. Not only did she not forget, she recounted the event with extra bells and whistles—it sounded as though I had nearly killed someone. "Yes," she said, "he's right here."

We were in my father's study, and I was standing behind his desk when I pressed the hot phone to my ear. "Hello, Baba."

"Hello, hello. And how are you?"

"Good."

"Lots happening, I hear."

"Yeah, you could say."

"So they verbally threaten you and now a train of cars outside your door. That's heavy stuff."

"I guess."

"Is it true what Mom says? You were in the kitchen with your gun?"

Silence. I decided not to lie. But before I could say anything, he cut me off. "So it's true then," he said.

"Yes," I admitted somberly. It was hopeless. I had pointed a gun at people.

"Well done," he said. "But forget pellet guns. Next time use *my* gun."

I was stunned. "The *shotgun*?"

"The twelve gauge over the bookshelf. You know where I keep the shot, opposite wall, bottom drawer. Listen, no bird shot either. The heavier the load the better. You can take whole cars out like that."

Before I had a chance to sink into the deepest grin of my life, my mother wrestled the phone out of my hand. "What shotgun? Are you insane?" she screamed. "He nearly killed us as it is. Have you forgotten he's ten? This isn't some cowboy-Indian thing; there's a horde of nuts circling the house trying to burn us down! Have you gone mad? Are you watching the TV? They just took Nassiri away, all deranged and bloody! Have you even stopped to think for a moment that maybe we're next?"

Part of me wished I had never thought of my gun, wished that I had cowered behind a couch and waited for my mother to use her mean voice on the perpetrators. A more compelling part felt heady with my father's affirmation.

Soon after, a loyal corps of officers came to protect us—pilots, colleagues, familiar and unfamiliar faces. They arrived with guns and took posts around the house and tried to calm my mother. "It's nothing, Mrs. General," they assured her. "The noncommissioned crowd's always been a thorn in our side. They've sensed some weakness from above and think this is their moment."

All night they sat in the entryway and Bubbi shuffled back and forth with trays of tea. In the universe of Iran, time may be measured by sips of tea, and that night the tea clock grew longer and longer as we counted the slow, doleful slurps that came from down the hall. We waited for something to happen—my mother and I from the living room, the officers from the hall, my father from his bunker, and a nation from whatever four walls had come to represent safety, or oppression.

The cars eventually quit their purposeless parade. The men's guns relaxed against walls. I took several unnecessary trips to the kitchen to gauge the situation and was struck by the *real* face of combat. I suppose I had expected wooden soldiers to come to our aid—identical men in bright blue suits and creased, white pants with wide, shiny belts. They would stand, tall and slim, next to their muskets and glow in the tireless shade of rose dabbed onto their cheeks. Instead, what I confronted was baggy eyes and the sooty shadow of overdue shaves. The officers had arrived in mismatched clothes, the habitual flight jacket thrown over a dress shirt, a service top with bell-bottom pants. They carried machine guns like they had ransacked an armory along the way. In the months ahead, the machine gun, with its distinctive splayed tip and artless frame of pressed steel, would fill the streets of Tehran and come to symbolize—along with army-green coats and blue jeans and half-grown beards—the face of a killer.

The next morning I opened my eyes to a house still standing. The cool, gray light that flooded my room muted all objects—the sketch of a desk or chair, the penciled-in Persian rug next to my bed with outlines of peonies and tendrils and medallion blossoms washed of their color. I lay in bed staring through the luminous gauze of curtains at thin streaks of leafless trees. There was an elusive answer in the air, almost touchable, and as I searched for it I realized I had lost the question.

I could not remember how the previous night's activities had led to this conclusion. How had I even made it to bed? When had I fallen asleep? Had everyone gone to bed at some point, agreeing to retire their torches and guns for a more civilized time of day?

I ambled out of my room in a daze and entered the living room, where my mother was conversing with General G, my father's deputy and acting commander of the base.

"Well, hello there, soldier," said a jovial General G. As a term of endearment, "soldier" had run its course.

"Good morning, General," I said.

"I hope you haven't let yourself worry too much about yesterday's theater. See, we have men on this base who are here to serve and who are loyal to your father, and we have a bunch of actors who keep us entertained. It gets boring otherwise." He turned to my mother and succumbed to a pair of boyish dimples that claimed we were fine.

"We had our own show," my mother was quick to note. "If you had seen soldier boy last night, your jaw would have dropped."

"Nothing less than amazing is what I expect from the general's son," said General G graciously.

My mother gave me a couple of playful pats on my butt and sent me away. "Why don't you go and get dressed, Mister? New day. New battle."

It was tacit that resuming a normal day and going back to school were put on hold. We had begun a new chapter in our lives and nothing would be the same until the story's resolution.

Through General G we learned that we were barred from leaving the base. The NCOs had a stronger following than anyone had thought, and it was unwise to test our luck at the gate: Taking us could tip the scale in their favor and radicalize the movement. It was safer, it was decided, to stay put where we could be defended along with the house, which stood as the most visible symbol of the power structure. "And if it blows out of control," General G had told my mother, "I'll fly you guys out myself. But it won't come to that. The boys are trying to figure out who the rabble-rousers are. We'll have this settled shortly."

He had barely left the house when the threats resumed. My mother seemed more emboldened. "Listen closely, chicklet," she told someone on the phone, "I'm not going to take threats from a couple of adolescents who've somehow ended up with stripes on their boogered sleeves. What are you waiting for? Let's see who's man enough to carry through, you or me."

With all the officers gone and my mother taking a nap, I felt the same loyalty to the base as before, and again I mobilized. I took my gun to patrol the house, running around from one parted curtain to another to see if anyone was close. Bubbi was an emotional wreck. "Put that damn thing away, you hear me? We gotta answer to God now. It's all over. It wasn't bad enough to be cooked in the desert, now they're gonna burn us. Oh, what did I do? I said put that away, ehh! You'll have hell to pay when Missus gets up. Don't believe me? You wait!"

Midafternoon, when my mother staggered out of her bedroom and saw me with the gun, I offered an explanation. "Don't worry, I haven't loaded it."

She turned away from me like she couldn't handle the added stress. "Anything new?" she asked Bubbi.

The short arc of the sun hastened the afternoon's rapid turn to dark, and a new anxiety set in. Men could attack under the mantle of darkness when we least expected it. My mother busied herself as before with a string of phone calls, and I took to polishing my gun on the sofa in front of the television news. For the time being, I had put my father's shotgun suggestion out of my mind. Climbing into bed that night, I leaned my gun against the headboard, set a box of pellets on my nightstand, and practiced a few times reaching for the gun with my eyes shut.

Morning. General G entered the living room dragging half of his body, steadying the swing of a compact machine gun, which hung off his good shoulder. My mother rushed to his side. "Oh my God, what's the matter?"

General G shuffled to the love seat, lowered his gun by the strap to the floor, and dropped back into the cushions with a heavy bounce. "Nothing," he said. He drew shallow, irregular breaths. "Stroke. Last night. Took out half the lights. Tomorrow? God only knows."

"What are you saying? You had a stroke? I'm so, so sorry." Seeing Mammad, who had led in General G, still at the door and fully absorbed, my mother turned to him and said, "Well, don't just stand there. Go get the general some *tea*!"

"I'm sorry, Missus. At once."

"G dear, I don't know what to say. Miriam must be beside herself. You shouldn't be walking around. Why did you even come? We've got to get you to the city, to a specialist, to Doctor—"

"Shh!" snapped General G. He reassembled himself like a collapsible doll that snaps back from mush with a push of a button and whispered, "It's a stupid ruse. Listen! The situation is dire; they've got the base. The doc's getting me airlifted out to Tehran, and you guys have to—"

"What do you mean, 'they've got the—'?"

"No time. You guys have to find a way out. Tell the general my hands are tied. But be careful; they're watching the phones, and they've got the gate covered."

In my father's dichotomous world, there were those who faced danger statistically and took calculated risks, and those who were scaredy-cats. The former were rare. Uncle P moved to London because he was a scaredy-cat. Anyone who was troubled by the uprisings, by strikes, or by NCOs was a scaredy-cat. Money sent abroad as a precautionary measure was a scaredy-cat move. And you were certainly a scaredy-cat if you wouldn't try switching from two skis to one. Sure, you'd fall; we all expected it. But the chance of a severe injury in water was minimal. General G's act had to be weighed against this backdrop. To me he reeked of scaredy-cat: No upstanding general would ever resort to such ridiculous role-playing.

Hearing Mammad's returning footsteps, my mother turned to me and pressed an index finger to her nose. The general fell apart again in his seat, and my mother carried on about the stroke with genuine concern. "What is the doctor saying? Thank goodness it wasn't any worse. You can recover from this; I know you can." No one could be trusted anymore. When the general was ready to leave, my mother called on two of the officers to help, and as they struggled to get the man to his feet, their guns swung against each other, got tangled with the general's own, and clanked loudly against the coffee table. "Forgive me, Mrs. General," one said. In the fiasco, General G let himself slip past the men and plop back on the cushions with all the dismay and helplessness of a sudden invalid. Buster Keaton would have loved it.

Though we couldn't leave, we weren't excommunicated, and my mother wasted no time formulating a plan over a tapped phone. Whatever she was saying to whomever she was saying it to was brilliantly cryptic. "There's absolutely nothing to worry about," she said. "This is our home, after all, and we'll deal with an upset like a family does. You don't sneak out of your house when there's a problem, do you? No, when you feel there's nothing else left to do or say, you rely on uncles and cousins for help. Then you sit down, have some tea, talk things over, and the answer comes to you. Right?"

That afternoon, Uncle P's cousin, M Dear, came to see us in a pitiful, dusty white Peykan—Iran's only domestic car, as common and uninteresting as a light pole. A 1950s Hillman Hunter at heart, the model was licensed for assembly in Iran with new trim and labels. But in keeping with English standards, it was cramped and sparsely appointed, a winner only in an uphill battle against the two-cylinder Citroën "lieutenant."

"Did they give you any trouble at the gate?" my mother wanted to know as she sipped tea with M Dear in the living room.

"No, not at all. That car's like a membership card," said M Dear.

"Oh, good. I certainly didn't want any of this to affect you. So what do you hear of P? Is he getting settled? I bet he's laughing at us now. How are you getting by with all the strikes? What do you hear on the street?" And on and on, gabbing about family and politics. Over the last few weeks, Aunt Z had decided to take a trip to London, to imagine a new life there. The conversation shifted to her. "She can't survive there. You might as well ask her to give up oxygen," said my mother. M Dear nodded.

On one of Mammad's returns with a fresh tray of tea and pastries, my mother said, "Tell Bubbi M Dear is staying for dinner."

"Yes, Missus."

"Oh, and tell K to take the rest of the day off. No point having him hang around for nothing."

"Yes, Missus."

I was infinitely relieved to hear M Dear was going to stay. While I took comfort in seeing loyal officers arrive to protect us at night, I was growing suspicious of the bonds of rank and uniform.

My mother distrusted Mammad more than anyone, and since he was the go-between who linked the kitchen to the inside world of the house, she had him banished to the laundry room with a stack of sheets and tablecloths to iron.

Mammad grumbled in the kitchen. "Let's make sure the sheets are pressed before they go up in flames!"

"Thank God somebody finally gets what I have to put up with in this house," said Bubbi opportunistically. "Bubbi, do this. But

Missus—Shut your trap and do that. But Missus. Who's to say this underling is another child of God? She eats like you, walks like you, and has got two words to say."

The irony didn't elude Mammad. Here he was, walking out with a pile of laundry that would occupy him till dinner, and Bubbi was sipping tea, yammering. "You ever stop to think, all you do is throw a bunch of things in the pot and light up a cigarette?" he said to her.

"If it wasn't for the shit I throw in the pot, you'd have nothin' to eat, you fool."

"And who's the fool who gets you your cigarettes?"

"Are you gonna stand there all day and flap your lips or get to work? Or maybe you're waitin' for her to call me and say, What's takin' him so long? Oh, nothin', Missus, he's in the kitchen flappin' his lips about two sheets to iron, sayin' no one does nothin' but put up their feet and suck tea."

Incapable of holding back his smirk, Mammad gave me a triumphant wink and pushed out of the kitchen.

The stillness of the house was not unlike that surrounding a massive sailboat caught in the doldrums. The dead float. The glassy water. The wait. Maybe a storm was brewing somewhere; maybe it was even headed for us; but for now there was nothing to do but calm the nerves and accept our predicament. M Dear and my mother had grown quiet, listening for the distant sound of thunder, it seemed, for a turn of fate.

"Let's move," my mother said suddenly. She grabbed a satchel and rushed to the kitchen. "Bubbi, grab your chador; we've got to leave."

I had no idea what was happening. My mother donned a chador herself, a black sheet covering everything save her face. The only other time I had seen her with a chador was when we toured the shrine of Imam Reza, the only one of twelve Shi'a imams buried in

Iran. Then, as now, the shapeless Islamic garb served as a guise, a way to pass as a commoner.

Bubbi came back with her chador, mumbling. "What's happenin'? They here? Allah have mercy. Missus, tell 'em I didn't do nothin'!" As we squeezed into the Peykan, she grew more curious. "But I can't see no one. Where're we going, Missus? God help us."

"Nowhere," my mother returned.

"Because I left the stew bubblin' on the fire."

"Don't worry."

We left the house and a few turns later took the long two-lane stretch that would terminate at the main gate. Noting this, Bubbi's curiosity was piqued. "Missus, the pot's on the fire. I turned the samovar to boil. In the name of Allah, merciful and compassionate!"

My mother had had enough. She whipped around and said, "Listen, and listen well. We're going to be at the gate in a few minutes. Those same people who wanted to burn us are going to be there. You even breathe and they'll shoot us. Do you understand?"

"Yes, Missus. *Allah-o-akbar*, God is grand."

My mother turned to me and said, "Take Poodie and crawl behind my seat. Get down low and not a peep, okay? And don't let her growl or bark." She pulled out another chador from her sack and handed it to Bubbi. "Here, make sure he's completely covered."

"But, Missus, it's gonna touch the dog. It won't be no good no more."

"Allah is looking the other way. Cover the kid before we get killed."

My heart started to accelerate as the car slowed down. Over the last four years my father had demanded and enforced a strict gate protocol. The interrogation applied to everyone, frustrating Mr. K, who had to answer to some measly soldier when he drove me to school and back. Drives into and out of the base with Baba were tense moments for everyone. Any favoritism or laxness would send the general flying out of the car. He'd grab the attending guard by the ear and roar in his face. "You're not here to graze. STOP, EVERY, SINGLE, CAR. Shoot them if you have to. Is that clear?" That hard-fought order was now poised to take us down. Though I knew I could keep quiet, Poodie remained unpredictable. Would she yap when she heard an unfamiliar voice? Would I be blamed for it?

We rolled to a stop, and M Dear cranked down his squeaky window. The tight squeeze in the wheel well made the tremble of the car seep into me, making it hard to know if I was shaking the car or the car was shaking me. What if the revolutionaries noticed the shaking mound behind my mother's seat? Wasn't it a given they would at least tell us to get out? And what then? Did we have a plan? Would M Dear peel out and crash through the gate? Did he know that Baba had authorized them to shoot?

In the few seconds that held our fate in the balance, I had a hundred thoughts. They were broken abruptly by a voice. "God be with you, Brother," it said.

"And you," said M Dear.

And we started rolling.

I resurfaced a few miles out. My mother slipped the chador off her head and began cheering. Even Bubbi succumbed to a silly grin, countering it embarrassedly with "But I left stew bubblin' on the fire!"

We spent that night with Mr. B, a poet of some repute, and in our paranoia, we used nothing but two candles to light his house. Mr. B belonged to Aunt Z's club of obscene friends, and his forte was wordplay; he was equally adept at fabricating bawdy quatrains as at quoting Hafez or Sa'di or Rudaki or one of the other greats on command. The top of Mr. B's head was completely bald, an attribute he claimed was a result of being smart and sexy. What Mr. B lacked in hair he more than made up for with massive muttonchops, a booming voice, exclusive Lark cigarettes, which he sometimes smoked two or four at a time, and a compendium of jokes, seedy ballads, and general balderdash. On the night of our escape, in the sallow light of the candle in the middle of the dining table, he tried his old charm with poor results. Fear ran through us.

Before daybreak, my mother shook me awake. "We've got to go," she whispered. "You can sleep in the car." We were off to Tehran in Mr. B's big blue Chevrolet. I had taken the land route only once before, accustomed instead to flying there. Some weekends, my father and I would get into his Bonanza runabout and head for Tehran. He would point us in the right direction and tell me to climb to a certain altitude. "Stay clear of those peaks," he'd say and promptly fall asleep. Once, when my long list of questions revealed my anxiety, he reassured me that my piloting made our flights much safer than if he were by himself. He slept one way or another. As I look back on it, all I remember is the approach of the hostile, mountainous range, my tight grip, and passes that get narrower and narrower.

On the road I knew much less what to expect, but then no one did. As we traveled north, we encountered one roadblock after another and a litany of questions. Who were we? Where were we going? Why? Unlike the military checkpoints we had grown used to, the makeshift stations of cement blocks and sandbags and the scrap pole or lumber that blocked the road were manned by young men, some no older than my teenage brother.

Mr. B was quick to recognize the opportunists for what they were, dangerous enough to stop for but, for now, powerless. *Where are you going, Brother?* "To Tehran, to collect my brother, Brother," replied Mr. B. "They burned him, Brother. They hung him. They shot him and beat him. Can you feel the pain of a brother, Brother?"

The Escape

What's your relation to the sisters? "I'm that sister's brother-in-law, and this sister's brother, which makes her my real sister, Brother." *God be with you, Brother.*

Bubbi and I sat at the opposite ends of the Chevrolet's capacious backseat—she peering out of her window, I intent on my view. A gang of clerics with machine guns peered down at us from the rooftop of one seminary we passed. Was this what they meant by an all-seeing God? I would have given anything for my usual vantage point in the sky, where God's gaze landed on us like benevolent rays of sun.

Our road trip, which would have taken an hour by air, lasted all day. By evening, when we finally reached Tehran's southern edge, we were greeted by a logjam of cars, grotty storefronts, masses of people, and pairs of men on motorcycles weaving past us, waving guns. We had the disoriented impression that we were traveling at high speed when in fact we had stopped and people were zipping past us. Some held the front page of a newspaper overhead. They stopped to plaster it on our windows, headlines that read, "End of Oppression." This Tehran was a far thing from my mother's snow-capped version of the city. I shuddered. We were entering a circus with all the animals running free: crazy, humorless.

Tehran's poorer south was inarguably full of people for whom the revolution was most promising. Any change would be good change for them, and given the revolution's self-promotion as the people's movement, it was hard not to read between the lines. *Which* people? These people.

We crawled past another emphatic crowd, and they slammed their fists on the Chevrolet's dining-table hood, screaming, "Death to the shah!"

Nervously, my mother turned to Mr. B and said, "Where's a Peykan when you need one?"

Realizing his American car was a liability, Mr. B stuck his bald head out the window and started shouting, "DEATH. DEATH. DEATH." Then, more quietly inside, "Death to all sons of bitches who sing a flea-bitten mullah's tune."

"Don't joke around. They'll hear you," said my mother, pulling her chador tight around her face.

"Are you kidding? As long as I have Mrs. Haji next to me they wouldn't dare. DEATH, sons of bitches, DEATH."

But Mrs. Haji couldn't save him. In just a few months, Mr. B would land in jail, along with other open critics of God's government.

9

My Own Revolution

It felt miraculous to reach Grandmother's street, to climb the steep hill and come to a stop in front of a little white tile with a hand-painted "۴۴." Four, the numeral, had always reminded me of a soldier at attention, ready for Baba's command. I used to think it was befitting we should have a pair guarding Grandmother's house. The numbers now pointed to a childhood ruse.

I rang the intercom and Mamman Ghodsi's voice came on.

"Yes?" she said in a dejected tone, like she expected anyone but us.

"Mamman Ghodsi, it's me. We're here!"

The gate buzzed open, and I ran into the courtyard, flying into my father's arms as though I hadn't seen him for years. He hugged and kissed my mother, too, whose joyful tears made my own unstoppable. Mamman Ghodsi wrapped me in her floppy arms and wept. Her cheeks were streaky pink, her nose a bright red, and she kept weeping long after we had settled in.

I tried to calm her. "Mamman Ghodsi, why are you still crying? Look, we're here!"

She whimpered back, "Sure, but what if you hadn't arrived?"

Perhaps she saw more clearly than anyone that it was suddenly possible to leave but not arrive.

* * *

143

Our move to Tehran could not have been timed any worse: We arrived in the epicenter of the revolution, on the very day the government collapsed. For the few days before our escape, the capital city had been utter chaos. Army barracks and police stations had come under attack, weapons circulated freely, and prisons had been opened. Bullets flew day and night at any perceived symbol of imperial establishment. On the night our house was surrounded, the prime minister had called the air force command post where Baba was stationed to order an aerial strike. Baba refused. Early in his career, he had been assigned a bombing run—napalm dropped on Qashqai separatists who had taken refuge in the mountains. He had swooped down over the encampment, locked in on his target, and at the very last second decided to drop his bombs two hundred yards too late. It was then he decided the air force would never act against its own people.

Several days after we moved in with Grandmother, I stumbled out of my bedroom to find her sitting on the couch, assembled in one of her floral dresses, tangerine lipstick in place. She was whispering to herself. At the dining table sat my father, resting his head in one hand and peering out the window over towering mountains to the north. "Good morning," I said to them. They faced me, considering what to say.

Was it morning?

Was it good?

The day's paper lay on the coffee table. The front page was covered with a photo of four bodies in dark pools of blood. "Ex-Shah's Accomplices Shot," announced the banner. I read their names. I read their names again. General Naji, who used to visit us regularly in Isfahan. General K. General . . . I felt hot. My face was burning.

My mother sauntered out of her bedroom in a peach robe. Her face showed no sign of worry, none of the frown she'd succumbed to in the course of the ordeal on the base. She approached us with a placid smile and said, "What's going on here? You'd think some-one's died in this house! Let's put on some music. Where's Bubbi? How about an omelet, everyone?"

Grandmother nudged the newspaper in her direction.

Moving to Tehran when we did may have been senseless, but at least we were together. I was to start school immediately, despite not knowing whether all of my family members would be alive when I arrived home. Maybe I'd return one day to Mamman Ghodsi and her ethereal prattle.

"Where is everyone?" I'd ask.

"Everyone? Everyone is gone, my soul. One by one. It's just you, me, and these four walls now. Walls to contain us so we don't melt away."

At some point I lost count of the demons that visited me at night. I'd wake up in a cold sweat to find Bubbi asleep like nothing had changed. She still made her bed next to me, on the floor. My grand-mother's house was cavernous, and at night I dared not leave the room I shared with Bubbi and my cousin Mimi. She was the prod-uct of my Uncle Hussein's teenage hormones. Grandfather had decided to raise her himself, as his own daughter—a scheme that worked until his untimely heart attack.

The room adjacent to ours was Grandmother's: ceaseless snor-ing. In time, I came to appreciate its earth-shattering regularity. I'd jolt out of bed to a distant rap of guns, only to be calmed by Mam-man Ghodsi's dry, open mouth.

My father and I met the headmaster of Kiasat the day after the killings. With the perfunctory interview and tour of the dining hall and some of the classrooms out of the way, my father wrote a check. I was expected to jump in with both feet. Maybe Baba wrote two checks, I couldn't tell, but I got a spirited welcome. The headmaster addressed me with undue respect. "You know where my office is now, young man, and I want to be notified if you have any problems whatsoever. Kiasat is proud to have students of your caliber." He lavished praise on my father and showed sanctimonious concern for the political situation. "The mob is out of control, General. They're after the very throne! But can they recite a line of Hafez to save their lives?"

Such was the rooted assumption, that rule was the rightful property of all those who could recite poetry.

Starting a new school mid-term posed its own problems. How would I be accepted into a competitive private school after years of absence from the system? With the exception of my short stint at the base school, my education had been the product of an American program in the mornings and Persian tutors in the afternoons. But admission was a simple process of knowing people who knew people, and here again, as soon as I began, it was clear to everyone that I wasn't your average rich kid.

I had never really had to prove myself. The American program was laid back, and at the base school where I was "the general's son," I was practically royalty. Here, in a city seized by revolutionary zealotry, where any authority was deemed corrupt, status was a liability. It was better to be an unknown without privilege, but I also knew how *that* panned out.

I don't know how I managed to survive those first days at school. Between the ride from home to the alley that led to the school's gate, I'd turn into soup, delivered to the frenzy inside a fenced-in yard. The headmaster had made an exception when it came to my uniform—"Not much is left of the school year," he had said to my father, "please don't concern yourself with such details"—and I desperately wished he hadn't. How much easier it is to pretend to be a bee when you are yellow and have black rings on your tail. As it was, I found the dress code strictly enforced at morning lineup. A teacher would grill one of the students standing four feet away from me who had a plain, white button-up instead of the school's logoed version, but she'd walk right past me, dressed in my silk turtlenecks, cable-knit sweaters, and corduroy pants. It was just a matter of time before I heard it: "How come *you* don't have to wear one? Think you're important?" And I had nothing to say.

This was the most inopportune time to be special.

At recess, gangs of rowdy students would surface like waves to ravage some unsuspecting kid. I expected to be beaten, punched in the nose, pummeled. Then they'd dissolve into a sea of white shirts, gray slacks, black neckties. Minutes later an administrator feigning urgency would rush outside, ask a few questions, round up some people, and the rest would be handled in the office. Tiffs were settled with stamps in demerit booklets, and it didn't matter whose. Word was, once your booklet's dozen boxes were filled, you were gone.

My teacher was Mrs. F, a middle-aged, Turkish woman. She was fair-skinned, large-boned, plump, plain, and gullible. Her sense of fashion was deplorable. Dark, glimmering gowns, big emeralds glued to her earlobes, a brooch pinned too far up or too close to the middle of her chest, and black pumps, always pumps, painfully twisted to accommodate her enormous feet. In class, bent at the knees, heels wobbling with each step, Mrs. F tragicomically chicken-walked the length of the blackboard and back.

Relegated to the class's back row, I had to contend with two simultaneous narrations, Mrs. F's and my neighbors', who cooked up one prank after another. If I weren't careful I could be pinned with their shenanigans; maybe they'd even frame the new kid, I thought. Then, if I seemed too informed, I ran the risk of being suspect, the snitch behind Mrs. F's allegations of wrongdoing, the one responsible for so-and-so's demerit. With my attention divided between these two worlds, I lived in the perpetual fog of not knowing what was happening. What page were we on? Would

I be called on to answer something? What were the kids launching now? Would the trajectory implicate me?

The leader of the back-row pack was Ali, an irrepressible short kid with bouncy, auburn hair and a puckish grin. Ali was one of the better students, which had to do, in part, with his specious excuses and broadly plausible answers. Mrs. F didn't have the patience to call him on his b.s. and instead commended him for having something to say, *even if* it wasn't what she was after.

Ali contrived various high jinks, launching paper planes in the middle of a lesson, booby-trapping seats and door handles and even chalk with chewing gum. He had a notorious repertoire of sound effects—not so loud as to offend Mrs. F but enough to trigger waves of laughter. He would deliver his homework without his shoes on and take bets on whether or not Mrs. F would notice. "How much would you give me if I made everyone leave class right now?" he asked one day. It seemed impossible and those around him started digging in their pockets. He wanted to see the money. "All right, all right." He made out like they had convinced him against his will. "Mostafa," he whispered, "take the money." (Mostafa was Ali's henchman.) Reaching in his bag, Ali produced an egg, casting a glance from eye to eye to make sure we understood that what was about to happen must later be attributed to his singular genius. The egg went flying toward the middle of the classroom, up, and *splat,* a stink bomb that sent us running for our lives with pinched noses. In the hour it took the janitors to clean the mess, we were relocated to a chemistry lab, where Ali and his cohorts wasted no time stuffing their coat pockets with test tubes, tongs, and Erlenmeyer flasks.

After a few weeks with my back against walls, trying not to accidentally look at someone the wrong way, I broke down one morning and realized I just couldn't face the impending doom. Standing in my pajamas I made an impassioned but unintelligible plea to be taken out of school and gave into hysteria when I detected no sympathy from my father. He repeated his question, stopping his shaver to face me, "Is there a cause? Has something happened?" and in between sobs I'd manage a pitiful "No."

"Why don't you want to go back then?"

"I can't."

"Why not?"

"Because . . . I can't."

"Well, there has to be *something* wrong for you to want to forego the rest of your education. Imagine you are an adult and you come to me and say, *Baba, why didn't I get beyond fifth grade? Why am I selling cabbage for a living?* And I say, *Well, one day you just couldn't go back.* Do you see that your request is a little unusual?"

"No!"

I stayed home that day and helped Bubbi squeeze peas out of pods. I cleaned herbs. We were having fish for dinner and Bubbi was gutting it. Her meaty hands slid a thin knife into supple tissue, in front of two little ventral fins. I was expecting the fish to protest. To pop. To expel its innards all over the counter. But nothing happened. It revealed itself without a fuss. Bubbi let me scoop out the animal's organs with my bare hands, and as I tore out its slimy viscera, I almost shrieked.

She clawed the purple heap of guts off the counter, leaving a limp carcass on the butcher block, seemingly fish, but unable ever to be one again. And what wonder lay there. Dorsal freckles a product of calculated placement. Forests of green on its back. Ruddy sunset sides fading to a creamy belly. The seamless transition of skin and scale to translucent tail fin. Eyes, real eyes with opalescent pupils and dark irises and eyelids, not the crude circles I was used to drawing. Lips, chin, forehead. Gills, the feathered pages of a delicate story.

"Pull over," Bubbi said, and her cleavered hand chopped off the animal's head.

The next day my father took me to school, and we went straight to the office. "It appears that Kiasat isn't the hospitable place we had imagined," he said to the headmaster. "Perhaps it is our initial impression that has faltered and not the place."

I had no idea what he was saying, but the headmaster seemed appositely concerned by this news. He began sententiously, "The young are attuned to the most subtle messages, a gift we lack as our senses get more and more jaded—guarded, you might say—with age. Mr. Aria's impressions are doubtlessly correct and we owe him our deepest apologies. You know, General, we aim to see the world as they do, yet we fall short. It's a constant battle to maintain that freshness." Then, in a dramatic gesture that said, We are in fact going to get to the bottom of this, right here, right now, he reached for his phone and announced with a voice of godlike authority, "Get Mrs. F from her classroom."

Why Mrs. F? If anything, I felt I'd landed in the middle of a rain forest. My father's inquiries into the problem amounted to questions like, Which of the species is disturbing you? Is it the beetles? The mites? Is it the moss? How could I convey that it was the whole damned mess? I just wanted to go back to living on an air force base in the desert.

Mrs. F knocked and entered with her arduous stride, bent knee and all, already apologetic: She even begged our pardon for sitting. The headmaster said she needed to do more for her students, and she agreed. She regretted not having done enough. He said we faced a crisis and that the school's survival was on the line. She couldn't agree more. Fundamental changes. *Indeed*. A shakedown. *Essential*. One of her students was unhappy, he declared, and I felt her eyes fall on me for the first time: Ah, so you're the reason I'm here!

"But I love Aria dear like my own son. I swear it!" she said. "I have his best interests in mind. He can attest to that. There is a connection between us. I felt it the first day I met him. I'm sure he agrees. Has anything in particular happened?"

The headmaster equivocated. "The details are immaterial. It's a matter of policy."

"Of course," said Mrs. F. She studied me.

The generalities continued. Effusive apologies from Mrs. F. More platitudes. More remorse. And so the matter came to a close. Mrs. F went back to her unruly class; my father returned to his troubled air force; and I was reunited with the back row, who were already steeped in plans for their next assault.

At the beginning of lunch hour, Mrs. F asked me to stay behind.

"So this is the way it is with you . . . you and the Man out to get poor old Mrs. F. They haven't found a smaller wall than mine to crumble. Is that it?" In a hostile tone, Mrs. F proclaimed that in the future we would deal with our own problems. There was a chain of command in the classroom, much like in the armed forces. "You should be familiar with that. Soldiers don't go crying to the general, do they? Any future mama's-boy stunts," she guaranteed, "will make the rest of your life here a living hell." And I wholly believed her. This simpleton is no simpleton, I thought. She was vastly capable and terrifying. "From now on you'll be my *mobser*"—the teacher's aide charged with maintaining order.

My heart sank.

At the end of the day, the teacher announced she had appointed one of us the *mobser* but that the person's identity would remain hidden. "For those of you who are fond of making trouble you should know that my *mobser* is my eyes and ears. One suggestion that so-and-so is mucking up my class, and I'll see to it that you're gone. Mark my words. Things are going to change around here." Mrs. F was pitting me against all my peers.

As much as I resented being used by those who had my "best interests in mind," there was one beneficial outcome: My new appointment gave me the protective shield I'd been seeking—mess with me and you're messing with Mrs. F. Since I was undercover, I didn't have to deal with the baggage that came with the position. Outside school grounds, a *mobser* turned into a loathsome worm, detested as a sellout, avoided like the plague. But if pushed, I could deny the appointment.

Still, seated in the back row—ground zero of mischief—I faced a predicament. It was just a matter of time before I'd have to report to Mrs. F.

One morning before Mrs. F's arrival, Ali and the gang were enmeshed in some sort of whispered conference. The class was full and characteristically awash in chatter: groups of two or three deep in gab, a flurry of things thrown back and forth, people rushing around, a squawk here, a caw there. Friendless and envious of the various cliques, I studied my classmates like I was hovering above the room, watching my own past.

Ali waved a latecomer closer. "Hurry! I can't say it from here. It's one degree above top secret," he said.

There was no effort, it seemed, to keep the plan from me. It was related in a loud whisper right next to me. Mrs. F's chair had been replaced by a defunct one, found in the hall with broken legs. Ali explained that he and the boys had placed it strategically so Mrs. F wouldn't have to pull it back. "She'll plop down first, I'll bet my life on it, and then . . . fireworks!" Then, as if to confirm that I'd gotten it, the mastermind turned to me and said, "What do you think? Will it work?"

"What?" I squeaked.

A guilty hush spread with Mrs. F's arrival, a sweet kind of guilt that started every morning, guilt over having been too loud or for having thrown a balled-up sheet of paper across the room or for using the last remaining minutes to finish homework. Mrs. F hobbled in wearing a nondescript black dress, feet spilling around tight pumps, one arm cradling a faux alligator-skin handbag, crazy hair fluffed in the front, squashed flat in back. Like a geisha she was heavily made up. I noticed for the first time that she looked tired and dejected. And I felt sorry. Why hadn't I ever seen Mrs. F the woman, Mrs. F the mother or wife? I started thinking of how she had squirmed in the headmaster's office, of the way he degraded her in front of me and my father. And for what? It was cowardly of me to have brought my father to school, cowardly to let the headmaster blame my teacher, and to watch Mrs. F take the fall.

As she neared her desk, part of me leapt to her rescue; the rest stayed paralyzed. Ali looked on, unflinching, a gambler who had risked all his chips. The spin of the roulette wheel. Mrs. F walked around her desk. Dropped her purse, stack of papers, and books on the desktop. "Get your books out," she snapped without looking up. Then, as if to say this has already been a difficult day, she surrendered all of herself to the chair. It wobbled. She tried to recover in a hopeless attempt that sent the two propped legs flying, she and the seat plunging out of sight and against the floor in a crescendo of metal, linoleum, and woman. In a fraction of a second, the teacher was sprawled under her desk, skirt lifted so the whites of her inner thighs lay exposed, encircled in flattened ellipses of black lace.

The classroom erupted. Girls rushed to the scene, and the back row began to convulse, Ali in tears. I felt my face drain of blood. Six or so students pulled Mrs. F out from under her desk, back to her feet, and the woman left us weeping, bobbing grotesquely on every other heelless step.

The rest of the day there was ceaseless talk of Mrs. F on the floor. "*Bad bakht-e khar* [the unfortunate donkey], you should've seen her face the moment before she went woosh! Grabbing at the air. Rolling on the ground." At recess the story spread. By day's end it verged on legend.

The next morning the headmaster plucked me out of a busy corridor and led me into his office. Mrs. F waited there.

"I understand that Mrs. F has entrusted you with a crucial job," the headmaster said. "It's a testament to your excellence as a student and a measure of how much we value you, Mr. Aria. Yesterday, as you painfully witnessed yourself, an unfortunate *event* occurred. I call it an e-v-e-n-t and not an a-c-c-i-d-e-n-t because we know that someone replaced the honorable Mrs. F's seat with another. To embarrass her. To mock this school. To further lawlessness. To bring the streets into the classroom. You can talk to Mrs. F privately and tell her what happened. She'll report to me, and we'll make an appropriate decision regarding the perpetrators. What do they think we are, turnips? My regards to the general. These are hard times. Your father's a brave man."

With that I was left alone with a fragile Mrs. F. She began by telling me about her injury. She almost broke her hip, but luckily it was merely bruised. She could hardly walk, she whimpered. Thank God luck was on her side and she wasn't permanently disabled. She conversed openly with God about the fortune of having picked me to look after her, to thwart the efforts of those who wanted her dead. "What is this world coming to when students want their teacher on the floor? Where dogs belong! Who was it? Who is the devil's aide? Who is it that wants to see a mother disheveled and disparaged? Is it not enough that I give 'em everything I've got? The best education. You are all my children."

A moment passed during which I said nothing, listening sympathetically.

"Oh, I hurt all over," she groaned, shifting her weight on the chair. "I can't stand, I can't sit, I can't lie down. I'm an invalid." Then she gave me a list of names. "So who was it? You can tell me. You're not only my *mobser*, you're my son. Just think you're speaking with your own mother. Those hooligans have done it this time. Wait till I get my hands on them. Tell me, which one of them was it?"

My eyes rose to meet Mrs. F.'s. "I don't know who did it," I said.

She looked confused, a seasoned poker player misreading a sure hand. A long few seconds passed, our eyes locked, but then, to acknowledge my position, she said meditatively, "You don't know who did it."

"No." I knew full well she saw right through me.

With more clarity than I'd ever had, I saw that I had been manipulated all along. And I wasn't going to put up with it any longer. It was unfortunate that Mrs. F would not meet justice as a result of my discovery. It didn't even matter to me that I would be turned over to a higher authority. Perhaps my father would be called in. He and the headmaster and I would sit in a closed room until I named names. But I knew I wouldn't. I felt pride in my position; I would lie to the very end. Nothing could shake me of this resolve— not that buffoon headmaster; not even the general himself.

Class resumed more subdued with a sulking Mrs. F at the helm and a gloating Ali in the back. During one lunch period, Ali called me over to pair up with him in a game of cavalry. Two contestants, one on the back of the other, challenged a second pair. There were no rules; your team won if you brought down the opposing rider. Ali hopped on my back, latched on to some part of his counterpart, and I started spinning. I was surprisingly good as a horse. I took an occasional punch in the head or a foot in the ribs, but I held on. Soon, Ali and I "rolled" them into a "pipe"—a technique so effective, henceforth it became our trademark and my nickname. "*Looleh* [Pipe]," Ali would say with a swagger, "you ready to roll 'em up?" And we'd charge—"Dig your graves, you bastards," he'd scream. "Me and Looleh are gonna show you hell." We became the reigning champs. Kings of cavalry. Blacktop aristocrats. Sure, there was a stigma in being ridden; I wasn't blind to that. But to go from nobody to Pipe was an achievement I was deeply proud of.

My playground association with the gang proved fruitful in the classroom. I congratulated the bunch on successful disruptions and once in a while even engaged in some benign but unruly act myself. For a week, Mrs. F wept off and on, at odd moments, and then left, never to be seen again. Was I to blame? I'd gladly trade culpability for the safety I felt in the company of my newfound friends. In her place we were assigned a long-legged, lean, self-possessed man with a quick tongue and a head of thick, wiry hair. He was young, arrogant, and sprightly, moving around the classroom with unnecessary speed in tight polyester pants, hips leading the way. He was always ready to pounce on someone for anything that smelled like a challenge. Undoubtedly he was warned about us. In contrast to a roosting Mrs. F, our substitute lived at the blackboard, a mirror for his narcissism.

The New One (one of many names we coined for the instructor) invited confrontation. His lack of compassion and apparent disdain for youth foretold the grilling we'd receive if he ever caught us in any act of insubordination. But this didn't deter the wily. Quite the opposite.

In the middle of our first English lesson, the New One asked if anyone knew the language. I shot up my hand and announced that I spoke a variant, "American." He let out a hysterical, hyenalike laugh, and said he hadn't heard of such a language. With great insolence, I declared that there was a country named A-m-e-r-i-c-a in which the language was prevalent. The back row burst out laughing. *Zarafeh* [Giraffe] called me to the board to draw a map of the world and show the class where "this A-m-e-r-i-c-a" was situated. And so I did, as well I could, which was probably not bad for a ten-year-old obsessed with maps. But he kept me at the blackboard. "How can you call yourself an American when you omit Florida and Alaska? Where's Indonesi, Hindustan, Escande-navi? Or do Americans not recognize anything else outside their borders?" *Amaleh-ye Cheshm Chap* [Cross-eyed Manual Laborer] proceeded to give me a lesson in geopolitics. "America is America because of England, that's why *English* is spoken there. There is no 'American,' because your beloved A-m-e-r-i-c-a was nothing before the English settled it—a big jungle with a bunch of bare-assed redskins running around with four feathers in *their* head calling woo, woo, woo, woo. Maybe you mean you speak *their* language." With that, I was dismissed, and though clearly dog-faced, I received congratulatory pats on the back as I made my way back to my seat—accolades from my peers, which mattered more to me than any historical accuracy.

As I was finding my place in the political hierarchy of fifth grade, the revolution's victory raised new questions. Precisely who was in charge? Who would control an armed public with a penchant for vigilantism? What of the feuding factions that had put aside their differences temporarily to topple the king? In what possible future could their varying utopias be realized now that old animosities resurfaced? And the question of God came back as never before: How was God responsible for the bloodshed? Ayatollah Khomeini, who had served as the aging figurehead of the revolution, quickly appointed ad hoc committees and tribunals to carry out Islamic justice—a code no one understood at first. In the first month after our arrival in Tehran, hundreds were arrested, tried, and shot.

The city was awakening to the aftermath of a tantrum: Buildings and walls were covered with bullet holes; windows shattered; cars flipped over; soldiers and policemen roaming the blocks in partial uniforms with nothing to do; women in billowing chadors floating across the streets, ghostlike; young men on motorcycles waving pistols; "conscientious" lunatics directing traffic with pointed machine guns. One enterprising man had turned a bit of sidewalk into a shooting range—one toman per shot and you got to keep the homemade targets he had drawn on notebook paper.

The revolutionary contagion spread through our fenced-in microcosm as well. The administrators came to represent the imperial regime, the headmaster the despot, and teachers, the vassal subjects of oppressive overlords. Detecting weakness at the top, students grew bolder with riskier pranks, more visible brawls, and rock throwing. The demerit booklet was useless now. Eighth-grade wannabe revolutionaries speculated openly about how much my father had embezzled, or how he was probably in cahoots with the shah's sister for such-and-such commercial privilege. I was shocked to learn they knew anything about Baba.

"I'd tell your dad to hide if I were you," a tall, pubescent boy told me one day, as though offering me insider information.

It was one of the last bitter days in winter when I rushed to relieve my bladder during recess in the dim, dank bathroom tucked in the corner of the playground. Normally, I would have used one of the stalls inside the main building, but I had waited too long and was desperate. The facility hadn't been cleaned for weeks, and the dirt and trash were likely reminders that order and cleanliness and teachers and banks and ministers and kings were a good thing.

Carefully, I shuffled toward a tall urinal, already unzipped. A soaked, black-and-white picture of the shah lay over the drain hole. The ripped-out page was one you'd find in the beginning of any textbook. I looked for a stall free of such desecration; after all, the king was still the commander of all the armed forces and my loyalty to the air force had not changed.

No luck. The vandals had defaced every urinal and toilet. Pictures of the shah floated everywhere, distorted, already a dream.

As steam rose off the arc flowing out of my body, I faced the horror of defiling the shah. I was lightheaded. I shut my eyes. Urine splashing against porcelain. The carnal elation of relief. And then I experienced a conflation I could not hold back. It was joyous to urinate on the king.

I opened my eyes. And aimed.

10

Turning Rotten

A week before spring, with daffodils and hyacinths already in bloom and the buds on cherry trees signaling the arrival of the Iranian new year, Nader was killed. Nader, our blue-eyed ace of the skies, founder of the Golden Crown aerobatic team. A 1950s black-and-white photo depicting Iran's first aerial acrobats occupied a prominent place in our house, alone on an ornate French Provincial side table. It was a quiet shrine. The photo captured a beginning, maybe of time itself, and the men who had ushered in the new era. The pictured pilots knelt next to their helmets in the diamond pattern they formed in the sky—Nader shaping the sharp point, Baba, his wingman. There were harrowing tales of close calls, near misses, and in-flight collisions. I had memorized them: Nader leads the Crowns in a low-altitude barrel roll, finishing a few hundred feet above treetops in southern Tehran. When the jets are right-side up, Nader notices a hole to his right—Baba missing; he's stuck inverted, controls frozen, plunging into the canopy of trees. Dead silence. The pack's listening for the unmistakable thud of explosion. "Mickey, you still with us?" Nader calls out.

Four years later, Baba had taken over as team leader and instituted even bolder aerial stunts. The day he had opened a show with his hair-raising "bombshell" maneuver, the two men exchanged looks no one understood. *What of death? Does it pertain to us?*

New Year's Day. The first day of spring was a scene of toys and kisses. But also of mourning. Should I have been excited that our Santa clone, Uncle Norooz, had once again snuck in at night to leave me presents? Somehow it seemed shameless to pretend. I thanked my mother instead for the wind-up motorcycle man that came with ten feet of adjustable, looping track, and she looked at me ruefully, as if to say, I'm sorry it has to come to this. She stroked my cheek with a distant stare, and her eyes filled with tears.

When we lived on the base, a sense of longing had permeated our lives, a yearning for family and friends, who, for the most part, lived in Tehran. Now, here in Tehran, together at last, the best we could wish for was a return to that sweet longing. For the New Year's holiday, my parents used to make a point of flying to Tehran and seeing as many relatives as possible. On my mother's side, there was Mamman Ghodsi and her ancient brothers—Uncle Dear and Uncle Colonel. There was Uncle Hussein, my mother's brother, and his family. All of Grandfather's left-behinds had to be visited. On Baba's side, there was Mother, Uncle Ali, my two aunts, and all their sons, daughters, and grandchildren. From house to house, cake to cake—by the end of the school holiday, my cheeks were a permanent lipstick red, and I felt dizzy, unsure who belonged to whom or how I was related to them. And if my parents couldn't make it to Tehran, they'd put me on a Hercules cargo plane to visit the family by myself. After takeoff, the navigator would climb down to ask if I wanted to visit with the crew, and I happily agreed. Up the vertical ladder to the cabin and a second one to the top bunk of a bed behind the pilots and I would swing my legs and study the switch-studded cockpit.

The Hercules framed the world with a dozen or so little windows. They were scattered around its lunar face, the eyes of a big, clumsy beetle lumbering through the air, magically aloft. True to its name, the Hercules made other aircraft appear gnatlike in comparison. It was wide-bellied and stout; its tail rose four stories off the runway; four chunky turboprops rumbled a slow, beetle buzz, whereas other planes whizzed or whined or screeched by in a hurry. A row of levers with little white balls on top stood between the pilots, and once in a while the captain nudged them all forward or pulled them back, maybe to know that he could, and you could hear the engines surge or settle in response. Invariably, cargo men were gamblers, and if they weren't dealing cards in the cabin, they were honing their pranks—flipping the back hatch open midair to confuse the technicians or locking the navigator in the bathroom.

"Mr. Aria," the captain would say, "don't go telling your dad we just goof off up here. Jamshid is looking for the enemy right now, aren't you, Jamshid? He'll get to it as soon as he finishes his tea." And the three of them would cackle.

Of all the personalities in Tehran, one stood out. Uncle Hussein (or *daee*, as one's maternal uncle is called) didn't fit any prescribed role I had known. He was Mimi's father but acted like her brother—she even called him by his first name. He was the hoodlum counterpart to my upstanding mother. And he was a wayward boy to Mamman Ghodsi, who still had to keep a vigilant eye on him. Daee Hussein had left a sprinkle of dents in the plaster wall, just inside Grandmother's entrance and, once in a while, got us kids together to show us how. He would hush us, wind himself up in a karate pose, and punch the wall, leaving yet another imprint of his knuckles.

Mamman Ghodsi's voice would stretch around the house then to sour the triumph. "Hussein, quit it. Was your father from the south side? Is your mother disreputable?"

"I've got to go, guys," Daee Hussein would say and sneak out.

He was a marvelous mess of things, but he was very convincing at whatever role he *chose* to play. I loved to watch him shift back and forth between the various familial and social strata. He was pals with the kids, respectful of the established adults, hip with the teenagers, buddies with the chauffeur, and always favored by the kitchen crew, who snuck him cream puffs, cucumber-and-feta sandwiches, or *tah-deeg* (the layer of rice at the bottom of the pot, crispy and oily and always in short supply). With our move to Tehran, he became more of a fixture in my family, triggering dormant memories I had of him, images that surfaced one day like a dead body in a mist-blanketed lake.

I was four and Grandfather was still alive. I heard Daee's low voice begging Mamman Ghodsi behind the patriarch's watchful eye, "This'll be the last time, I swear to God." He kept an eye on Mamman Ghodsi's little embroidered purse.

"Leave the Lord's name out of this. Haven't you dirtied things enough?" she said.

Daee took her money weeping, saying again and again as if to convince himself, "I swear this is the last time. I swear it. I'll come clean. You'll see."

For Mimi, Daee was a headache. In the first ten years of her life, she had been led to believe he was her brother—Grandfather's save-face measure to erase the damage caused by his teenage son's love child. When Grandfather died of an early heart attack, Mimi became inconsolable, and my mother broke it to her that her father hadn't died, that, in fact, her father was her brother.

For my mother and Aunt Z, their brother had a karmic affliction—he was destined to find trouble and to be beaten by Grandfather for it. Mamman Ghodsi described her only son as "one of those charlatans" or "one of those creatures." And for everyone else, Daee Hussein was "certifiable."

In those first few months in Tehran, I got to see what everyone had seen for so long. I learned firsthand why Daee Hussein had acquired so many dismissive labels, but not a moment with him lacked excitement. He was reckless, that much was a given, and he wouldn't last two seconds under my father's risk-management regimen. But I found myself attracted to him precisely for that reason. I was also getting excited by the urban anarchy and the revolutionary songs on the radio. I hated to think what this said about me.

One night Daee took us kids to Luna Park, so named after the amusement center in Coney Island. Along with the concept of an amusement park, the attractions were completely imported from the West. Popular among them was the Ferris wheel, whose peak gave a dazzling view of the city. The cars moved gingerly up and down to the lazy spin of the wheel, and an array of blinking bulbs stretching out from a central hub called, Come to me.

"We'll be able to see all the city from up there," said Daee's wife.

"Garbage!" said Daee. "The kids want fast, they're looking for a thrill, smashing things, rides that throw you around. They've come out with their daee for a good time, not to go on a ride that massages your hemorrhoids."

But Daee's wife insisted, and we got in line. Though the limit was four per car, Daee Hussein paid a little extra to get all six of us in with the claim that he was wiry and the kids didn't really count. Packed tight, we moved up one rung at a time as the operator stopped the wheel to unload and reload his cars. We rose all the way to the top, and there we stopped—something was going on below, we couldn't tell what, and we sat motionless. In other circumstances we might have gloated at being the topmost car, suspended above all the rest, enjoying the unimpeded view. But Daee was not inclined to enjoy quiet views. He started shouting in the direction of the operator: He was getting a nosebleed, he said; he was claustrophobic and had to pee and couldn't hold it anymore which, he stressed, was a problem for people below us; he said his wife was pregnant and was having contractions; that the moon's gravitational pull was lifting him off his seat; he had an epileptic son on the verge of a seizure. We dangled over Tehran in a skeleton of angle iron, swishing back and forth in a black night until Daee ran out of warnings.

The man had a fear of keeping still. He began to make the car swing. Our screams egged him on, and he climbed out and to the top of the vessel. The operator below was bawling at the sight of one his cars ridden by a deranged passenger. Only when the wheel started moving again did Daee get inside. "No ride with your daee," he turned to me, "is a dull one. Remember that."

A month into our stay in Tehran, Daee Hussein gave me a switchblade and taught me how to use it—"Forget Hitchcock movies. No jabbing. Look, like this, forward, slice, forward, slice." I had heard of "knife pullers" from the south side, but they belonged to a fantastic world in which honor and respect formulated life-or-death propositions. These men never called the authorities. They settled tiffs their way, by the blade.

Every morning before school, I'd slip the knife under the elastic of my underwear. In the few minutes it took for the cold blade to assume my body temperature, I faced the thing I was becoming, the boy I was leaving behind. The only person I ever told about the knife was Ali, who was fond of using it to carve his name on any surface. It was a curious thing to do, I thought, chiseling your name on school property. When I questioned him, he said, "If they can see Khomeini's face in the moon, then they can also believe that Imam Ali has reappeared to scribble his name everywhere."

One day, studying the knife, Ali asked me, "Looleh, don't you think the dodos in the office will hang you if they catch you with this thing?" All my life I had been good, or played the part anyway, and here, overnight, I had turned rotten. I could imagine doing anything, but what I feared most was confronting my father. It was just a matter of time before my deviant path ran into the general.

Rotten people, I was learning in Tehran, see the world as more complex. I gathered that Bubbi stole money from Mamman Ghodsi. I had unknowingly caught her in the act times before—I had seen her on countless occasions snooping in Grandmother's bedroom, snapping shut her little purse just as I appeared on the scene. But in Tehran, I was no longer falling for her "innocent" routine. No, I intuited the bare truth: an awkward clench of fist, the nervous upper lip.

I noticed, as well, that my cousin Mimi had grown breasts, the type men leered at. I didn't really respond to them—ours was a deeply fraternal relationship, and they were simply unexpected. It was, rather, the man-breast dynamic that I saw and understood.

At the time, Mimi was taking biology, and her textbook was filled with pictures I loved to leaf through. Invertebrate anatomy. The digestive system of mollusks. The sexual organs of a flower. The human penis, even mine apparently, was a network of tubes and bulbous organs with curious names like epididymis, seminal vesicle, and vas deferens. Mimi explained what looked like the head of a ram as a woman's reproductive system. "This," she said, "is the uterus. These two are the ovaries." She moved the tip of her pencil to the model's crotch, "*vagine.*" In the next few minutes she laid out the entire process. I heard about "the male reproductive instrument" and "insertion into the canal" and "seed transfer." The picture became painfully clear. From then on, any male-female relationship had, in my mind, an opportunity for seed transfer.

Once, I caught a glimpse of a poster taped to the back of Mimi's closet door: a bereted man sporting a black mustache and wispy chin hair. I was curious to know who he was, but Mimi threw the door shut, leapt back, looked around to see if the coast was clear, and scolded me. "You didn't see anything," she snapped. It was a strange reaction from someone who'd always trusted me, and she realized it. "It's Che," she whispered sheepishly. "He's the answer."

I saw she was moved by something holy. There was sanctity in her voice, fire in her eyes. She ranted—revolutionary rhetoric, exalted things, words I associated with the macabre world of the night, with the roar of guns, edicts on the lips of an executioner. Her final tirade drained the blood from my face. "If your dad sees this, it's the end of me, the end of us all."

When Mimi was away I'd visit Che. There was no greater symbol of my moral turpitude than this illicit face in the bedroom. I'd leave the closet door open, prop myself on Mimi's bed, and study the poster as if I had to come to terms with my own face in the mirror. What an indignant face, rebellious and assured. The jargon on TV and on the radio aimed to ground the revolutionary outburst in an ideology; they made a case for an *Islamic* republic. But there was a wholesale truth to the revolution that went beyond any single group's claim. Freedom and independence—and their fearless pursuit—had a universal appeal. It was written on Che's face. I found myself drawn to it.

At ten, I had turned into a lowly knife puller, looked after by a seasoned thief, protector of a revolutionary who happened to be my closest companion. I had walked into a thick fog and emerged on the wrong side. I imagined facing my father and having to explain how I got this far.

While I was grappling with my new predicament, my father petitioned for and was granted early retirement. No one thought he was any safer for it, but at the very least, it meant that the air force no longer cared to hold our old household goods hostage. One day, movers arrived with the life we had abandoned. Since our arrival in Tehran, I had lived out of a suitcase, and all the things we had left behind belonged to a different life. Distracted by a new school and the rash of executions, it had not occurred to me to ask about our old home. As far as I knew, the NCOs had set our house on fire. Now, the contents of my youth—toys, favorite sneakers, pellet gun, memorabilia—were parked in front of Grandmother's house.

The dust-covered trucks recalled our final days on the base. The threats. The swarm of cars. *Next time use the shotgun.* How I'd crouched behind my mother's seat, trembled at the gate.

While the movers discussed how to get everything into the vacant flat above Grandmother's, I peeked around the front gate and found a trailer connected to the last truck. As soon as my eyes fell on the load, I remembered the goodness that had preceded the revolution. Confusing tears covered my face. How could I have forgotten my octopus dune buggy? The car stared at me playfully with its big, bug-eyed headlights. For a moment, I felt I could leave all that had happened, run to it, and pick up where I had left off. But then a sorrow settled in for a childhood that had to be cast away.

What Western media had hyped as the "collective will" of the Iranian people had devolved into opportunism and bloodshed. My mother resorted to unabashed denial; foreign media clung to American culpability: If the shah's government was guilty of human rights violations, then America had failed to use its clout to curb the regime's abuses. If the shah spent inordinate amounts on the air force, then American payoffs had lured him. It was easier to examine the dirty laundry of a superpower than to consider the wholesale shifts taking place with rooftop executions. In criminalizing cosmopolitan values, the clerics were driving an ideological wedge between modernity and Allah. And there was no question—by modernity they meant America.

Omid, who was attending a college in Connecticut, was calling nonstop.

"Yes, Baba is fine," my mother told him. "He's retired. He's completely safe."

"Is it true General J was executed?" he asked.

"Rumor has it, Nader punched the judge in the mouth. Maybe he grabbed someone's gun and shot some of them before they got him," she said.

"What about all the others? How do you know Baba's safe?"

"Your father hasn't done anything wrong. If he ever stands trial, they'll have to send him home with a medal."

My mother's account of the end followed a movie plot. Nader couldn't have been blindfolded, tied up, and shot. He had to go out with a bang. And as for the hero of this film . . . there was no way *he* could fall; he'd be returned to us decorated!

But by the end, even the most unassailable figures couldn't be trusted to stay alive. Baba and I were on one of our after-school errands, driving around Tehran's frenetic streets, choked now by postrevolutionary disorder. Motorists had become captive to street peddlers rushing around selling newspapers, cigarettes, gum, fruit, candy, toys, plastic ware, metal cans, slippers, baked beans, brine-soaked walnuts, hats, jewelry, wiper blades. It was as though we were driving through a general store. I had just paid for the day's paper from the passenger seat and was reading the headlines to my father, who seemed pleased that the tedious wait in traffic at least gave his son time to practice reading.

The paper was filled with the usual stuff—the hubbub of an uncertain government, the fate of the armed forces, a bomb that destroyed part of parliament, heavy pronouncements from the clergy, more arrests, more executions. And then, prominently mentioned on the lower half of the front page, *"Jon Vayne Mord."* *Mord* and *mard* are heteronyms in Farsi; I read, "John Wayne Man." Baba corrected me, *"Dead*, not man. He must have died." It was impossible. Absurd. The article described Wayne's movie career, his cult following, his battle with cancer, the film left unfinished—I wished desperately to stop reading, but my father was all ears.

I asked him when he had first seen John Wayne. When had the Wild Wild West been tamed? What were the chances of finding some unreformed gunslingers in the West? Were there any saloons left anywhere? And how had the movie star come to learn Farsi? By the age of ten, I could at least admit he was probably not Iranian.

Baba regarded my curiosity stolidly. He had first seen John Wayne's films in Alabama. The West was still wild. The chance of finding a gunslinger was good, especially in Texas, where it was common to find cowboys on mustangs lassoing cattle. There were no more saloons except on Hollywood sets. Worst of all, I learned John Wayne didn't speak any Farsi.

"What do you mean?" I said.

"John Wayne spoke English, which doesn't do Iranians much good. They could've used subtitles, I suppose, but then half the population can't read. Anyway, with dubbing you can create a better character for the character. Incidentally, the John Wayne *you know* is very different from the cowboy John Wayne played by the real John Wayne who wasn't a *cowboy* at all. Actually, he wasn't even John Wayne—his real name was Marion something."

I couldn't believe what I was hearing. What intricate lies I had been led to believe. All the games in which I'd imagined being the legendary cowboy with a southern-Tehran lingo. I'd say little, but what I said moved mountains. How many times had I faced some imaginary foe blocking my way out of my room? *Bekesh kenar joojeh* [Pull over, twerp], I'd rasp in Wayne's throaty voice.

It was all a sham, like everything else. A mouselike king. An impotent military. Mighty heroes falling like gnats. Public floggings. Kangaroo courts. The world had become rotten at the core.

11

The Chase

With her life sorted away neatly in boxes, safe, she thought, from the revolution, my mother left for America to calm my distraught brother.

"Do you *have* to leave?" I asked again at the airport.

"I know this is hard, my love. But we talked about it, didn't we? Your brother is halfway across the world, worried sick about Baba. I'll be back before you know it."

"When?"

"A week. Two at most," she said.

When she disappeared down her gate, I felt the tenderness of her lie. It was the same sweet assurance she'd been feeding my brother for weeks.

In her absence, the ladies with whom I spent the afternoons could be themselves. Since childhood, my mother had appointed herself the arbiter of propriety and decorum, and under her watch your every move was subject to scrutiny. Now, I saw Grandmother sitting cross-legged on the kitchen floor, in front of what appeared to be a small grill. I watched her rub something on the ball end of a pipe that she laid over glowing coals. When the paste began to smoke, Mamman Ghodsi sucked the fumes through the longish stem. She scraped clean the pipe, heated and reloaded it, all unhurriedly. Then she raised her languid lids to spot me. We studied each other. She managed a shadow of a smile before returning to her implements, and I gathered that she felt no earthly pain: No one could be shot; no one could disappear.

In place of my mother appeared Aunt Z, who was back from London to finalize her move. She reported that Uncle P had become even more pessimistic about the future. His advice: Cut your losses and run. For the brief time she stayed with us, I'd tag along with her as though she were a part of my mother, returned to me. She didn't seem to care and invited me along even when her motives proved questionable. I was the movie camera Aunt Z needed to perform her grand comedy. With everyone else fleeing, fled, or dead, a ten-year-old would have to do.

So I followed Aunt Z when she snooped into Mimi's room and snuck a peek at her diary. "Oh," she'd say, "we'll have to see about that." Then I trailed behind her and up to the roof, where Mimi often sequestered herself.

"So, who's this Esfandiar we hear so much about, you little devil?" Aunt Z asked.

Mimi shot back, "You ought to leave people's personal items personal."

"What *personal* items? Don't you see you just gave yourself away? You just confirmed that you know an Esfandiar, *and* that it's personal. You surprise me. This is the best you can do at sixteen? When I was your age I could juggle storms!"

Aunt Z turned to me, giggled, and repeated Mimi's words in a witch's tone, *You should leave people's personal things personal.*

For Aunt Z the revolution itself was a subject of mockery. A drive with her put a very different spin on the ever-present threat on the street. "Look at this bozo," she'd say of a motorcycle passenger. "I bet he thinks he's Colombo with that gun." She would roll down her window and taunt the man. "Make sure the safety's on when you holster that thing, Brother."

The Chase

I craved the lightness she brought to our dire situation, the audacity to take on anyone or anything. Whereas Baba always meant everything he said, you could count on Aunt Z to mean almost nothing.

Nothing moved her more than irony. Here was a nation, which, after fifty years on a Western tack, had decided to turn Easterly. If you didn't know any better, you would think our women always wore head-to-toe chadors. Aunt Z relished the about-face. All the elitist fashion slaves who'd fought to the top of their social circles with their latest Yves St. Laurents, Cartiers, and Lancôme preproductions now hid under macabre robes.

"How about accompanying your favorite aunt to the bazaar so we can get these hussies dressed right?" Aunt Z asked me one day. "They want a revolution? We'll show 'em a revolution." She winked, and naturally I went.

Close to Tehran's grand bazaar, you got the sense that those fifty years were a figment. We parked the car and set off on foot along undulating earthen walls, lumpy street, root-heaved sidewalk, and past beggars, crippled and deformed. It was as though they were in various stages of dissolution. The upper half of a woman was all that was left of one beggar. Another struggled to keep his head and arms up and out. Aunt Z stopped to stuff each outstretched hand with folded bills and whispered to herself, "Praise, Lord. Save him. It's all I ask." Neither God nor I needed to know whom she meant by *him*.

The bazaar was a sprawling network of corridors and covered halls, some ornate with their distinctive, ogee-shaped alcoves. The diffuse light that spilled in from the various cutaways in the roof caught still dust motes in the air, imparting a dreamy quality to the vignettes. Inside one busy shop we found an old proprietor. Presumably, he had once filled his droopy, faded black suit and white, slack-collared shirt. He wore a dusty fedora and stood in front of towering shelves filled with reams of black cloth. What were the customers examining? To my untrained eyes, the choice was black or black. But Aunt Z ruminated over a dozen different fabrics piled for her on a wide bench.

"I haven't been here for years," she said to me. "Would you believe it if I said we all used to wear chadors to leave the house? Mamman Ghodsi, me, even your mother, Mrs. Chanel. Here we are, back at the beginning."

She wasn't remorseful; she simply felt history more poignantly than the rest.

In the car again: "How are you doing? Can I get you anything?" asked Aunt Z.

"No. I'm okay." She had given me some money to hand to the beggars on the way back, and I'd grown pensive. Should I also have asked God to save my father? Whose God would I ask?

"I swear, there's something genetically wrong with your side of the family," Aunt Z said. "It's your dad's fault, of course, 'cause your mom's not like this. Why say no when someone offers to get you something? Why do you assume I mean a cucumber? Maybe I'm trying to give you gold. The right answer is, *What do you got?* Then you can decide."

"What do you got?" I said, proud of my quick recovery.

Aunt Z gave me the finger. "Too late, Mister. You had a chance at the crown. Now you'd be lucky if you got a fart out of me."

A quick stop at the grain store, closer to home. Aunt Z ran the car up the sidewalk, the trunk sticking into busy traffic. She was delighted to have found a spot in front of the store, even though it meant only half of the car could fit. "Let's be quick," she said, "or we'll have to massage someone's balls."

We pushed a fragile door open to find piles of burlap sacks raised neatly in rows, marking off three or four dust-covered pathways stretching away in different directions. The door swung back of its own accord and sealed us off from the street. Eerie quiet. Where were the customers, the proprietor? In place of voices haggling over price or quality, we faced an olfactory commotion—barley, rice, lentils, black-eyed peas, chickpeas, mung beans. I followed my aunt's timid steps on the slippery floor to a slight man bent over an open ledger. When Aunt Z spoke he lifted his head.

"Yes?" he said in a deep baritone as though answering a phone.

There was something peculiar about his manner. Still eyes. A calculated, delayed response to everything. A certain mystery lay behind the man's grave façade, like he knew something we didn't.

Aunt Z placed her order. "Kidney beans, favas, your best basmati."

"Oh?" he crooned. "And how much did the lady have in mind?"

Before the man's helper could fetch the order, Aunt Z made sure the storekeeper knew who we were. "Mrs. H's grandson," she said, pointing at me. With any merchant, securing quality was a matter of cultivating a long-standing relationship. To require the best basmati meant nothing; Mrs. H's name, on the other hand, opened doors.

"Oh," said the man. "Why didn't you say so earlier? And your eminent relation?"

"Her daughter."

"Well!" A smile stretched across the man's face. He turned to his helper and shouted, "Boy, bring me back that list. Mrs. H's daughter changes things. Such a distinguished emissary on such a trite mission."

The teenaged helper rushed off with the new order, and the man started jabbering about hackneyed political stuff—the shah was good for the land; people don't appreciate a good thing till they lose it; shooting themselves in the foot; now they've got to kiss the ground he walks on to get him back; won't they ever learn? You could tell it was for our benefit. And I detested it. I wanted to say, I am one of the ungrateful people; I am one of those who shot myself in the foot. Hadn't I peed on him? Wouldn't I do it again? But I kept my mouth shut.

When it was time to pay, the merchant left his desk and came back with a balled-up plastic bag, which he buried in one of the sacks. "Please," he entreated, "none of this is worthy of Mrs. H." I had no idea Grandmother shopped for anything, or that she was popular with grain merchants.

That same night, I followed my aunt to the unit above my grandmother's apartment, where our household goods were now stowed. With the exception of my father's makeshift office in the middle of what was the living room, the flat was a dark storage. It reeked of naphthalene. The place was filled with boxes, draped furniture, and a thirty-year collection of Persian rugs stacked two feet high. Like Baba's impassive façade, his sanctum said little about his inner turmoil: A quaint lamp hung over a partially uncovered sofa, its arm cradling a honey-colored guitar. On the coffee table, there was a clutter of sketchpads, pencils, and a small stack of books.

While rummaging in the boxes, my aunt and I were joined by a neighbor who was a regular fixture at Grandmother's. In the middle of their chitchat, I heard Mrs. X ask Aunt Z about the grain store.

Aunt Z dug her hand in her cardigan pocket. She pulled out a gummy, chocolate-brown cylinder the size of a roll of coins. "You mean this?" It was the contents of the bag the store clerk had stuck in the rice sack.

Like heroin, opium was highly illegal. It looked to me like Aunt Z was brandishing enough of it to sedate an entire neighborhood, not just Grandmother.

"The child!" said Mrs. X with bulging eyes.

Aunt Z cast a cool eye toward me and then back at her cohort. "Who, *him*? He's already corrupt."

After school, I would find Mamman Ghodsi in a doleful state.

Baba, who undoubtedly recognized the sweet, lingering smell of opium in the air, was eager to leave the house, waiting restlessly to take me on errands. Maybe he thought the end was too close to put his foot down, to banish drugs from the house. Maybe he couldn't bring himself to deprive Mamman Ghodsi of her only escape.

Before his return to Iran, Ayatollah Khomeini had promised mind-boggling things, and the more naïve had come to believe the revolution would bring free utilities and free gasoline. Instead, with the ouster of the shah, heating oil became scarce and power outages were the norm. Secretly, I had found the first half a dozen fun, the candlelight a diversion, like living in John Boy's world in *The Waltons*. With the lights out, we all climbed into bed at the same time, and the night felt bigger and quieter.

"Good night, Mimi," I called out into the darkness.

"Good night, sweetie."

"Good night, Mamman Ghodsi. Good night, Aunt Z."

Their faint voices came back from the adjoining room.

"Good night, my soul. May you dream of seven kings," said Mamman Ghodsi.

"Va, what kind of good-night wish is that?" Aunt Z started. "They'll arrest the kid in his sleep!"

"Baba, Baba. Can you hear me?"

"Alpha Oscar Kilo," he said.

"G-o-o-d-n-i-g-h-t."

"Yes, sleep well."

"Goodnight, Bubbi," I said finally.

"Damned be my pappy's pappy. No peace standing. No peace layin' down. There's gonna be no peace in my grave!"

Mimi burst out giggling, and I couldn't tell which I found more comforting, her nasal chortle or Bubbi's overwrought disaffection.

* * *

Aunt Z's permanent move to London was finally at hand, and she expressed a finality that left no room for happy lies about quick returns. It was as though a giant eraser were at work, rubbing away everyone I had known. All my so-called aunts and uncles had disappeared. My heroes were dead. And one by one, my loved ones were being taken from me. As they left, my landscape was shaped by mourning and anxiety. When would *he* disappear?

To keep my spirits up, Baba would take me on drives around the city to check on the progress of our house or to visit the chicken farm. We had some rentals, I learned. A plot of land. Did I know my parents had bought me and my brother two adjacent apartments in a clutch of new high-rises? "Let's check on the construction," Baba would say. "Village of the West," they were called, floating above the city, above the Eastern realities of the street. "Cyrus the Dolphin is starting a ball bearing import firm. We should go and see if we can't have them made here. Do you know how ball bearings work?" And we were off, imagining the three parts of a bearing in the gridlock of cars. Occasionally, we'd stop to sample the goods being offered us on the streets. Early melons weren't as sweet as they were made out to be, but there was a delectable immediacy in the experience of having one sliced open right at a vendor's cart that made me think this could well be my last melon with Baba.

One day, I asked Baba if we could take my car for a drive. The dune buggy was hidden under Grandmother's apartment building, collecting dust in the carport, but it was the only way to get back to who I was, to restore my father to the way I remembered him, to a time when our lives were shaped by our own imaginings. I wanted desperately to believe we still had control. Baba said it was a good idea. "Tomorrow, we'll take it in for an oil change."

The following afternoon we geared up in our full-face helmets, jumpsuits, and gauntlet gloves and walked in deliberate, heavy steps toward my car. The ladies lined up on the terrace overlooking the ramp, glum-faced and stupefied. On some level, I shared their mystified gazes—why wouldn't Baba hide like any normal, hunted person?

We buckled up. My father started the car, and the familiar loose clap of the VW's valves brought a grin to my face. Baba revved the engine, and the motor's rumble bounced off the walls and filled me with hope. As we backed up the sloping driveway, I waved energetically at the ladies. They shook their palms at us dispiritedly, as though they saw a different, disastrous outcome than the one we imagined. We were about to parade around town in a topless car with orange flames, air scoops, and a black octopus painted on its hood—a billboard that read, LOOK AT US—and if we were pulled over by any one of the autonomous militia units, it would be like meeting a death squad.

On the road, the car's effect was strange. It turned widespread rage into lighthearted curiosity. Some people laughed uncontrollably at the insouciance of a man who, despite unbearable realities, was out for a good time in a bright dune buggy. Some rolled down their car windows to ask questions. Children went mad, pointing, laughing, squirming, screaming, big-eyed and wonder-filled. I could tell we were followed, but no one stopped us. The barely disguised pursuits fizzled with cheers and whistles and flapping arms. When we made it home, Grandmother hailed the Prophet Mohammad and his heirs as though we had completed a trip to Qandahar and back on foot.

Later that evening, Mamman Ghodsi complained to my father. "My dear," she started softly, "in the time you were gone, our livers got kebabbed from worry. Do you think this is the best time to be seen in that creation?"

"Things aren't as lawless as they say," said Baba. "We mustn't forget that a central government is a relatively new concept for us, that for ages the people of this land have governed themselves according to a constitution codified first in a culture. I've no reason to believe I have offended the law of the land. Fugitives run and hide, my dear Mamman Ghodsi. We take proud steps."

Mamman Ghodsi nodded quietly, unconvinced.

After that, my father and I took the car out for a drive once a week. Fewer and fewer signs of distress accompanied our departures. It wasn't that danger of running into revolutionaries had ceased or even diminished; it was simply that one gets inured to unthinkable conditions. All was going well—Baba had a list of errands, and what better way to dispatch them than to zoom around in an open car in the fresh air of spring? On one of our runs he handed me the keys and said, "The owner should drive his own car."

"Me?" I said.

"I don't see why not."

Getting behind the wheel for the first time since Isfahan sent shivers down my spine. With the exception of my one foray into the city, all my driving had occurred on our base and then primarily off-road. Tehran was a different story. I could just imagine Ali and the gang at school: "Okay, Looleh, you and *your* dad took your car for a drive, and *you* were driving. Let me guess, then you took your jet for a spin?"

If the ladies suspected my father had lost his mind, now they were convinced. Baba took the passenger seat like it was the most natural thing to do and left the driving to me, never recoiling when cars cut us off or when I almost ran into people who did not heed my hand signals. The chicken farm was our destination, and I was fabulously excited: Not only did the drive put us on the expressway, but the farm required a minor off-road jaunt. Bubbi had already warned me not to bring any more chicks back from the farm, as they left droppings all over the house and ultimately died. But I couldn't help myself. Before we returned home, my cousin packed a few in a shoebox, and Baba tucked it between his legs and laid a hand over the lid. I started back, rolling over the stretch of gravel with an eye on the smoothest path for our delicate load. *These* birds, I determined, were going to live.

The farm's driveway ended at two paved lanes of fast traffic, which I had to cross to get onto the expressway. While we idled, waiting for a big-enough gap, I noticed a Ford Capri parked directly across the road, the type of car popular with young, revolutionary hotheads. Four men in jeans and army jackets scrutinized the passing cars. Two were standing, gabbing; one was sitting on the rear hatch with his machine gun on his lap; the driver was smoking behind the wheel. Was it just chance that we had to pass them? A trap, maybe, since there was no other way out?

"Carry on," said Baba. "Find a nice opening."

My car had one nagging problem which wasn't bad enough to fix and not small enough to disregard. Sometimes when you attempted first gear, you'd end up in third. There was no way to know; you just had to ease off the clutch and feel the difference. Consumed by the threat in front of me, I misshifted and stalled in the middle of the two lanes, staring the men in the face. Restarting the car and screeching away, I noticed the posse scurrying. Moments later, their Ford had caught up with us, and the passenger in the front seat was waving me over. I turned to Baba. He pointed at the approaching on-ramp: I was to take it.

But, Baba, they want me to stop.

So? I imagined him saying. *Do you stop for anyone who wants you to stop?*

I took the on-ramp, and for a moment, I thought the men had missed the turnoff, gotten stuck in traffic, and lost sight of us. But suddenly, there they were again, next to me, the passenger in the front shouting something I couldn't make out over the road noise. A look at my father escalated the tension: He pointed at the accelerator and then at the road ahead. There was no question—they were revolutionaries, and we were escaping from them. I picked up the pace and wove in and out of traffic, no hand signals, no looking twice before a lane change, just the road ahead and a wish that my pursuers would disappear. But the dark hood of their car edged next to me again. The front passenger's hair blew wildly in the wind. His face was twisted. I glanced at Baba and noticed he clasped the shoebox tightly with both hands. I knew what I had to do.

I floored the accelerator, and we careened around cars. As the speedometer leapt higher and higher, the car started to shake. I had done this before, on the runway of our air base. The disaster I sensed then felt familiar now, like I had imagined the terror of this chase. Who were we fooling? It was just a matter of time. They'd find him. And there was nothing anyone could do. I pictured the end of the expressway ten miles away. A set of lights. And here I was, speeding us there.

When the men moved a car's length ahead of us, I noticed their guns pointing at me. It was then that I felt the tapping on my knee. Baba was telling me to pull over.

This was my anguish. The haunting of my sweaty dreams. This was the gunfire that cut through the night. This was Allah's vengeance. This was Che's face. By the time the men surrounded us, I was already rehearsing Baba's capture. They would tie his hands, beat him, push him into the car. And I was the traitor who could do nothing but bear witness.

12

You, Too, Major?

It had come to this, the movie of the end of my life, which had so often played out in my mind. One man trained a machine gun on us; another waved a pistol back and forth, screaming bloody murder. I watched the tip of the handgun nervously, aware of how big a hole pistols leave in targets.

"And back there," the leader shouted at me, pointing behind us with his pistol, "I'm tearing my head off to get you to stop." Now at me, "I should've shot you. And what the hell is this thing?" pointing his gun at the car. "No lights, no plates, no doors." Back at me, "Gassin' up like that! What do you think this is, your own private road? The hell with the rest? I have news for you, Mr. Screw the People, we ran that shit shah out of the country. Those days are over."

The harangue continued, pistol pointed at me. I was fastened securely to my seat, and my face was beginning to burn in my helmet. The man spoke to me man-to-man, revolutionary to offender. I was reminded of an incident back on the base: I had accidentally strayed into the restricted zone; a soldier held me at gunpoint; I told him whose son I was, but he shook his head and said, "Never heard of no general."

Glancing over at Baba, I noticed he was looking skyward, struggling with his helmet buckle. No luck; he pulled off his gloves and tried again. The diatribe continued. Listening to the man, I was almost convinced that I was the reason there had been a revolution.

"You Savakis are all the same," said the man. "The Man behind you so you can get whatever you want. Now who's got the stick? You're good and accountable now!"

Hearing "Savaki" covered me in a cold sweat. Savak, the shah's secret police, brought back images of Evin and of scarred victims. The organization had become emblematic of all shah-era abuses, even a ten-year-old and his car.

With his helmet off, Baba smoothed his hair and said, "What's going on here? I couldn't hear a thing you were saying."

The man gave him a silent, baleful stare.

Following my father's cue, I unbuckled and pushed off my own helmet.

"Great Presence of Ab'bas!" said the leader, horrified. "How old are you?"

"Ten," I told him, sounding unsure. Until then, my age had been a point of pride.

"Ten?" He turned to Baba. "What in the name of God are you doing with a ten-year-old behind the wheel, man? Are you a crackpot?"

Baba objected. "He's actually a very skilled driver."

"I'm chasing a damn ten-year-old?" The man couldn't get over it.

"Ten, yes, but he's every bit of a truckhand, if not more."

Truckhand. It was one of those terms, like outhouse, that peppered my father's vocabulary as a referent to his lost time—and class. No one else I knew ever used "truckhand" or knew what it meant, but in the brimming chauvinism of the inner city, truck driver machismo was famed.

"That's great, but he's ten," said the man with the pistol. "Does that mean anything to you?"

"Why don't you take him for a ride? See for yourself. If you come back unconvinced, then we'll have something."

Incredulous, the leader turned to the others. "He's got a ten-year-old behind the wheel and wants me to go for a ride!" he said.

"Why take *my* word for it? You'll see what I mean," Baba continued, offering to get out so the man could take his place.

"Take it easy, Uncle. I believe you. The kid's a truckhand. You satisfied?" Perhaps the man was convinced he was dealing with a lunatic. He calmed down and reminded us of the legal driving age, the speed limit, the convention of pulling over for authorities.

"Authorities?" Baba spat back. "What authorities? When I see four men in jeans pointing weapons at me I run. How does anyone know who you are? Of course I'm not going to pull over. One look at you and I told him to step on it."

Realizing the futility of arguing, the man took a deep breath and said, "Let me have your license."

Baba was a general in all matters official. General in casual conversation. General on a reservations list at a restaurant. He was a general on documents and deeds. General when anyone called the house. General to friends and family. General on visits to America. General as though the title was his first name. And the rank was enough to turn these "authorities" into killers. By the time he produced his driver's license, I'd stopped breathing.

The man took a long look at the square piece of laminated paper. Then his eyes rose to meet my father's.

"You, too, Major?" he said.

The question was tinged with disappointment—that my father had turned out to be a minor officer; that a member of the air force rank and file, the cadre on which the revolution had relied so heavily, was breaking the law; that he had to back down. But what kind of divine mistake was this?

The man continued, conciliatory. "Please take this thing home,

Major, park it, and don't let the kid drive. We need you right now, Brother," he said, and they were off.

My father studied his license, shook his head, and slid it back in his wallet. We swapped sides and drove home. As we reached Grandmother's iron gate, I hopped out to ring the buzzer. Parked under the house, the car's booming rumble died with one last gasp.

"Why did the man call you Major?" I asked Baba.

"Funny," he said. He took out his license again, looked at it, and said, "I got it when I was a major." Driver's licenses in Iran didn't expire. They were likely renewed when someone's title changed, as when a major wanted to stress he was now a major general. But Baba had no concern for such influence. As a matter of fact, he considered self-promotion a sign of weakness. What you expressed on the outside was advertising for what you wanted to think of yourself—not what you were.

Who Baba was, what he had become, relied on pivotal moments early in his career when the head of the air force rejected favoritism and supported his talent. He felt indebted and made it his mission to find and nurture potential. But the truth was, the majority of those who were rewarded lacked any merit. Instead, they cultivated power through alignments, payoffs, and venal offices. The revolution was out to change all that, to trim the tall and stretch the short—no one's lights were ever to come on before anyone else's. But of course that romantic ideal proved to be an ephemeral blip, a quaint little dream to fill the chest and justify murder. The favored-class system returned with a vengeance, and this time God was there to defend the inequity.

13

Terminal Exam

The dreaded fifth-grade terminal examination was upon us, and it, too, had become a revolutionary tool to level the playing field. The lanky louse who had replaced Mrs. F reminded us that we were about to meet our end, that the test would pick us apart, one thread at a time, a carpet loom in reverse. "Only the deserving," he declared, "will stand. The rest of you will have the good fortune of seeing me again next year, and I the unfortunate luck of you. Maybe you'll drop out altogether and make it easy on everyone." It didn't matter how rich we were or what connections our parents brought to bear—the exam was destined to prove that we of influential families, we, the masqueraders, would make better porters and grocers than economists or ministers. There were rumors that religion would be a big part of the exam. All those incomprehensible phrases! Did we know which, *hejleh* or *hejrat*, was the pilgrimage to Mecca and which was the sanctioned night in bed with one's bride? Did we know the difference between the two forms of tithe, *khoms* and *zakat*? And who could even say what *tithe* was to begin with?

Of course, there was no way to study for the blasted thing. No study guides, no crash courses. Having only been told that the test was based on knowledge we ought to have acquired, I regretted the way I'd spent my last few months. Maybe I shouldn't have been

189

so focused on finding a place for myself on the social ladder of the classroom. Certainly, nothing good had come from my association with Ali and the gang. Pipe? A stupid nickname was all I had to show for it. With all the time spent in the American school system, I should have spent the last half of the year studying twice as hard. The real problem was not knowing how I ranked among my classmates. Were we all confused by the four forms of Z, or was I the exception?

My written Farsi was marginal at best. It was true I had received private lessons, but my tutors' eagerness to please Baba eclipsed any real assessment of my academic progress. "How is he doing?" my father would inquire in passing, and my teachers would glow at being addressed by the general. "Superbly, superbly. He's a phenomenon," they'd flutter and flush. That I had received twenties across the board on anything I had ever done before our move to Tehran was neither surprising nor comforting. I had a sudden realization that columns of perfect scores meant nothing; the great, equalizing exam was poised to deal with people like me.

In my previous life my mother made a production of any rite of passage—lost teeth, the first day of kindergarten, first grade, the first time I donned a Boy Scout uniform. She would haul out our family Qur'an, place it on a huge tray next to a bouquet of flowers and a little bowl of water, and have Bubbi hold the tray in front of me, in the doorway. I'd press my forehead to the holy book and then walk under the tray, and Bubbi would spill the bowl of water behind me for a safe return. My mother was positioned to take a few dozen pictures with her new Kodak, and if the shots didn't come out, well, it didn't hurt to fill the bowl and repeat the farewell. Now, the Qur'an was viewed with suspicion, and anyway, my mother was nowhere to preside over the rite. Her two weeks abroad had turned into two months, and I had overheard Baba on the phone quietly telling her not to return.

My father was not in the habit of recognizing firsts, made wary by my first day of kindergarten. He had decided to personally deliver me to the base school, but the drop-off had not occurred as smoothly as he had imagined. Seeing him leave, I started to scream and wail; I chased behind him and scaled the school fence with teachers in tow. In the end, he put his base duties on hold to conduct an official inspection of the facility until I calmed down.

But exam day would get no special treatment. "Big events force doubt," said Baba as he drove me to school. "But, really, you're no better or worse than you were yesterday."

I wasn't sure how that was supposed to calm my nerves; if anything, I was hoping today I would be a lot better than I was yesterday. Driving to the exam site I thought about the spilled-water ritual. Like Bubbi's burnt rue seeds, there was no way to make sense of it, but I still wished somebody had dumped some water behind me as a precaution. At school, we were loaded onto a bus and motored to the exam site, a block of concrete buildings fashioned in the modernist convention of spare adornments and slender parabolic windows stretching from floor to ceiling. I had imagined a mosque or seminary as the site of my undoing, not the kind of structure emblematic of the "disease" of forward thinking. The hundreds, no, thousands of kids gathered in the vast courtyard from area schools were separated via an efficient numbering system that would have made Eichmann jealous. The mirthless administrators led us to our assigned rooms through cool halls filled with crashing heels and a deafening hush. We took our seats and watched as the proctors marched down the rows and distributed our death sentences: wan stacks of stapled pages, upside down. After rigid instructions targeting cheaters—"you can be sure we'll catch you and throw you out by the ear"—there came a shrill command from a large woman at the head of the long room. "Begin," she said. Her voice rang like a fire alarm.

Panic. Everyone had begun, and I was still ruminating over the threat. For weeks, Ali and the gang had been busy thinking of ways to smuggle notes into the room. Mostafa swore his elder brother had done such-and-such and succeeded. Afshin suspected the revolutionaries were much savvier and that old tricks wouldn't work. Ali discussed the possibility of girls being recruited as informers, and Mamal insisted his sister snitched on principle—there was no need for any recruitment.

Now, here I sat facing a neat stack of white sheets, a charged Parker fountain pen, and absolutely no stirring on my part to put the two together. It was a peculiar thing, one's end. Any thought about reconciling the kid I had been with the kid I needed to be vanished. Neither did I find it troubling that I had a father whose expiration date had passed. The present was so wide and deep and eternal, I felt utterly lost in it or, quite possibly, found.

Heads were lowered everywhere at precisely the same angle. Backs were humped like neat furrows in a plowed field. Elbows jutted out uniformly. Pens hovered at some agreed-upon angle to the perpendicular.

I had missed the rehearsal and felt no remorse.

Before it was illegal for women to show their hair or bodies in public, before female newscasters were reduced to an oval opening of eyes and nose and mouth, there was a woman on TV who taught yoga in a black leotard and a wide headband that held her thick black hair against her egg-shaped head. In a funny accent, she guided her viewers through simple poses, which I loved to follow. "Now we push the leg ooop," and I imagined millions of legs all across the world rising in unison.

When a lady proctor slipped an arm around me and lowered her face to mine, whispering, "Start my dear, start," it was as though Yoga Woman had called the next pose. "Yes, thank you," I said.

Of what use are trees to society? read the line at the top of the first page. I couldn't believe it—I could list a thousand things related to trees and none of them had anything to do with religion. *In what way does mathematics help us?*—page two, another wonderfully neutral question. *In your opinion, what is our country's most important historical period?* This one was trickier; what if the grader was a revolutionary? Our own period was too risky—surely, I'd have to reference the shah. Maybe they wouldn't frown on Reza Shah's time, but then, he was not only the shah's dad but a dictator himself—harsh in comparison to his son. The twenty-five-hundred-year-old Achaemenian dynasty, the starting point in the shah's secular version of history, was equally problematic: Always it was Cyrus the Great or Darius or Xerxes who was glorified, not their achievements. I was stumped. There wasn't one thing I could think of that didn't involve a king. So I wrote about Persepolis, the capital razed by Alexander the Great at the height of the Persian Empire. My essay ran off-topic, but, in describing the ruins I had visited on several occasions, I could avoid the shah.

Unbelievably, then, I was looking at math problems. Baba had a head for numbers, and his math games had sharpened my skills.

"How many melons would we take home to Bubbi," he'd ask as we ate some on the side of a street, "if we bought all thirteen, gave half of them away, and ate a quarter of the remaining on the way home?"

I'd try to stall. "Don't you think that's too many to give away?"

"Okay, let's not give any away."

"But then we'd get a stomachache if we ate a quarter of thirteen melons."

"Is there a better way to quantify that?"

"Which? The melons or the stomachache?"

I had spent an inordinate amount of time on the essay portion of the test, and I raced through the remaining pages in what felt like a flash. Then, the shriek of the same woman who had begun this dream filled the room once more. "Pens down, pens down," she said.

It was over. With everything that had already happened, it was silly to feel this passage as profound, I knew this, but somehow nothing else compared. I was standing in the middle of an unimaginable future, safe from the ravaging anxiety of the exam. I felt giddy and light. I had imagined the exam as a monster, a growling, fire-breathing creature of the night. But, forced to face it, I had discovered it to be a big, snoring oaf. The future, it turned out, was a bluff, a weak hand constantly called by the present.

When the letter came from the Department of Education that I had scored 17.5 on the exam, I was so ecstatic I didn't know what to do. Not a perfect 20, but well above passing. I had spent a week buzzing around with an irrepressible urge to see the world anew, and 17.5 offered even more of a buzz. Baba's surprise proved to me that there really *was* something to be proud of, that he had not fallen for those inflated accolades.

High from the proof of my intellectual prowess, I started summer with less anxiety. The realities of life still lurked in the shadows. Our friends were dead; our future was on hold; and there was no indication that my mother was coming back from her visit. I hadn't forgotten my turn toward corruption. Yet summer break meant whiling away lazy mornings in the kitchen with Bubbi, drawing, or reading old copies of *Zanan*—a ladies' magazine—till Baba returned from his daily activities. He had enrolled in French, art, and guitar lessons. His new exercise routine involved riding a bicycle to his classes with the guitar strapped to his back. Midmorning, when Mamman Ghodsi and Mimi got up, I'd have a second breakfast, copious amounts of tea, and listen to *BBC World News* and the worried chatter over what we had just discovered. Our neighbor Mrs. X would stop by, and the somber mood would lift. She joked and gossiped, which made me nostalgic for a time when Bubbi's kitchen was a marketplace of rants and ribaldry.

Afternoons I spent running pointless errands with Baba, reading the newspaper to him in a traffic jam while Mamman Ghodsi tended to her opium. Once, when the Toyota Baba had recently purchased got a flat in a busy rotary, the truckhand in me jumped into full swing. I jacked the car up and replaced the wheel as Baba watched with a half smile. At home, I turned Grandmother's drab terrace into a great skateboarding track. And there was Mimi's sanctuary, the roof, to exploit. From there, I lobbed flaccid cucumbers and overripe pears onto the neighbors' properties.

One idle day, I had a brilliant idea. I would invite Mamman Ghodsi to a tea party in the back of the hatchback Toyota. I folded the backseats flat, spread a lace-bordered tablecloth inside the car, and stole some couch cushions, the fruit bowl, and two fancy dessert settings for the occasion. But for it to feel real, Bubbi needed to serve us tea and raisins and rock candy on the silver tray.

"Bubbi, please. Don't you miss having guests and making tea and everyone coming and going all the time?" I asked her.

"No. Thank goodness they're hiding."

"But Mr. B wasn't bad. Was he? You liked him. He told all kinds of jokes and made you laugh."

"I'm happy the way it is, with or without that bald man stinkin' up the whole house. Stuffin' four cigarettes in his fat mouth at the same time. Oof, so you explode!"

"Don't you miss Mammad and Mr. K and Hassan Agha the gardener and Ab'bas?"

"Miss who, *Pippi*? A man combing his damn mane like a dog in heat! The only good one was the gardener who burnt under God's sun and didn't never ask for two sips of water. My heart sizzlt for his soul. The rest of 'em were sons of bitches, every single one of 'em, starting with that K, bustin' open his gut buttons—didn't leave a pistachio in the whole house, that one."

"Please, Bubbi. It's probably the same distance from the kitchen to the car as it is to the living room. You won't be doing anything extra."

"If it wasn't bad enough to jump for the missus, I gotta dance for her ripened egg now. Where's two seconds' peace?"

"Please, Bubbi. Please," I said.

"Akh! This'll be the last time. You hear? I'm not bringin' no tea to no car party no more. My pappy be damned if I do. He's laughing at me already!"

Mamman Ghodsi was temperamentally positive and readily accepted the invitation.

"Is there time, my dear, for me to freshen up?" she asked me.

"Sure. Can you be ready in ten minutes?"

"An invitation like this demands a whole day's preparation, maybe even two. I would have to take a bath, call the salon for a *mise en plis*, have Mimi touch up my nails—"

"Your nails look fine, Mamman Ghodsi. I'll have the driver pick you up in half an hour," I said.

"Make it an hour, my life, and I'll see if I can't run a hand over this wreck of a ship."

In the end it took Bubbi, Mimi, and Mrs. X to lift Grandmother's buttocks and thighs over the bumper as I tugged at her from the inside. With one knee in the car and one still unaccounted for, Mamman Ghodsi threatened to wet herself, and I rushed to the back of the car to take matters into my own hands. I pushed past the ladies caught in a silly fit of laughter and heaved the rest of Grandmother over the lower lip of the open hatchback.

How I remember her festive gown, her glowing face, tangerine-colored lips, and Soir de Paris scent as though she had arrived for a ball. Mamman Ghodsi was a queen at heart, and no indigent condition could change that. She gave me tremendous hope I could lose everything and still be myself.

"Mrs. H," I feigned in the manner of a treacly host, "it would bring me great pleasure if you would allow me to peel you an orange."

"How can I possibly refuse the product of your sweet fingers, Mr. M?"

"You must forgive my humble home. The salon is uncomfortable, and this chandelier—" I pointed disapprovingly at the car's dome light.

"What this dwelling lacks, my soul, it amply makes up for with love."

"You are too generous, Mrs. H, especially since you had to enter in such an undignified way."

"Speaking of which, have you given any thought to the manner in which your whale of a guest will have to be craned out of your cozy nook, so filled with your delightful company and attendance?"

"When I am in your presence, Mrs. H, the last thing I want to think about is your departure."

And we burst out laughing.

14

No Generals Left

Before Mimi fell in love and out of sight, she and I used to wander down to the best-known department store in town and listen to sappy love songs by the Eagles, Bee Gees, and Gloria Gaynor, whose hit song "I Will Survive" seemed written for Iranians like us. The toy department was inundated with cap guns, phasers, and clattering tommy guns, and while I had never tired of anything that shot projectiles or rays, I found myself wanting nothing to do with guns. It was more interesting to shop for bras. Women's undergarments hung in the open, in colorful displays of peaches, violets, lacy blacks, and soft ivories. There were padded bras and huge ones and demi cups and even bras with flaps, which Mimi said were for nursing. I wondered why no one had thought to add flaps to boys' underpants.

As weeks passed, there were fewer and fewer reasons to visit the department store. Its imported merchandise started to dwindle. The shelves began to empty. Nothing new or up-to-date was offered for sale. Time, it seemed, had stopped with *Hotel California* and first-generation color TVs. My new pastime was giving Mamman Ghodsi makeovers, which she tolerated despite the lengthy production and resulting mess. Using risqué colors, I turned her into a bordello operator. As *Madam* Ghodsi, she bit one corner of her lower lip, raised an eyebrow, and threw me a coquettish wink. "Like that?" she asked earnestly. I shook with laughter and she joined in, ruining my work with her tears.

In my repertoire there was Mamman Ghodsi, the attractive sixty-some-year-old bride with cheesecloth draped on her face. Heavy green eye shadow transformed her into Frankenstein's ghoulish partner, lips in purple, nostrils blackened wide. Chaplin required a good dose of eyeliner, penciled-in eyebrows, pale foundation over the cheeks, and a hat made of cardboard and a plastic bowl. Mamman Ghodsi's natural shuffle resembled Chaplin's. Best of all, she could become a vampire with tousled hair, shadowed cheeks, and blood running from the edges of her mouth. "Where're you takin' the ketchup bottle?" Bubbi would grouse, but when she saw my creation she let out a gratifying "Heee! My heart stopped," she said. "What in the name of God did you do to her? I thought my pappy's pappy had come for me."

When Mamman Ghodsi first saw herself as a vampire she burst out laughing, and I had to explain there was nothing funny about it. "You have to suck people's blood, you *have* to, you can't look at yourself in the mirror and laugh, because it's what you are."

I set to work on my own face. I matched Bubbi's smattering of facial moles, wrapped a paisley head scarf tightly around my head, strapped on one of Mamman Ghodsi's hefty bras stuffed with two oranges, and donned a collage of mismatched dresses, vests, and pajama bottoms. I morphed into a village bride, a female general, a tramp.

Perched on a kitchen stool, Mrs. X gave me theatrical advice. "Now swing your bum; make it like you've got something we want. Now work your breasts. More hips. That's right, side to side. He's got you down pat, Bubbi," she teased, and even Bubbi simpered. "Can you see Agha walking in and seeing him like this?" she said, worried, and I secretly wished Baba would show up, to see that I wasn't what he thought I was. I had changed. I was undependable and free.

Baba was getting antsy. Four months after the revolution, the land he had served—improved, he would say—was quickly devolving into dogma and provinciality. And there was no sign of a government to halt the decline. The emerging winners of the revolution were not the secular nationalists thought most likely to restore order, but, rather, the politically ambitious mullahs under Ayatollah Khomeini, the self-proclaimed moral voice of the revolution. Having secured the courts, they ruled with impunity. One turbaned judge boasted that he personally administered the death sentences he authored. "Corrupter of the Land"—the verdict required Baba to repent his most cherished accomplishments.

"Tomorrow," said Baba one day, "we'll go waterskiing. How does that sound?"

I was curious to know where, in the middle of Tehran, one skied.

"The Karaj dam isn't far. We have a clubhouse there," Baba said.

"*Who* has a clubhouse?"

"The air force. It's time we find out what it is about retirement people like so much. And what kind of a retirement would it be without skiing? What do you say?"

"Sure, I guess."

The next morning after breakfast Bubbi had a beach bag ready for me, along with instructions.

"Here, look, I packed a lunch for you and Agha, and here's a watermelon, trail mix for the car, a few boiled eggs, and a bunch of fruit. Tell Agha not to buy nothin'. I'm still tryin' to do something with the wagon of melons you brought back the other day. Tell him we're not on no base no more. And don't ask for nothin' on the road either; you know he can't say no to you. You'll get diarrhea if you eat that shit, you hear? You'll be up all night crappin' your pants, and who's got to clean it? Me, that's who."

Mamman Ghodsi had gone pale. As we were getting ready to leave, she approached Baba and said, "Do you think, my dear, this is a good time to ski? It's so unsafe to be out, and going back to the air force, I mean, what if someone were to recognize you?"

"If we can't ski, my dear Mamman Ghodsi, what else is there left to do?"

The twisty, mountainous road we took to the air force clubhouse was the same one my father and I often took to snow-ski. But now, without snow, the landscape felt foreign and hostile. It was as though the soothing white veneer had hidden the true craggy nature of things. The slopes, so graceful in winter, were blackened in stark shadows. Jagged rocks. And trees, vicious trees, sent their roots into any crack or fissure, splintered the shale, or jutted out of looming escarpments. Rocks the size of houses teetered above us; loosened, they could flatten us. We were following a river to its dammed source, and as we pushed farther and farther upstream I could tell it was getting angrier—a rolling, frothing fury.

I wished I could have shared my father's joy at seeing the concrete wall of the dam and the lake behind it. Wall-like mountains lined the edges of the ominously still water. We could have been looking at a vast bed of onyx or at tar or ink or—

"Baba, are there animals in the lake?" I asked.

"Sure. It's known for its trout."

"Do trout bite?"

"Nibble, maybe."

"Baba, I'm serious."

"If you mean, do they bite humans, then no. But I imagine they use their mouths to masticate."

"Are there any sharks in there or killer whales or sea lions?"

"You think I don't know my saltwater animals? Very sneaky, you."

"How about alligators then?"

"Okay, maybe a couple of lost alligators. But only two."

"Baba! Are there or are there not any alligators?"

"Alligators principally favor warmer climes, and this water, as you can deduce from all the snow that feeds it, is nippy."

"How nippy?"

"Close to freezing," he said. "It's very exhilarating, actually."

"Is it true that when hypothermia sets in, you feel warm?"

"Yes."

"Then how would you know you're freezing to death?"

"You don't. But what difference does it make? Real or imagined, if you feel warm, then you should try to enjoy it."

Pulling onto a discreet driveway brought us to a fenced gate shackled with a heavy chain. A few flat buildings, fifty or so yards down the driveway, stood by the water's edge. In front of a quiet bank of docks, two maroon ski boats sat tethered. They looked as if they had petrified into the lake's granite surface. Baba waited quietly, looking over the facility and the still water. I knew that look well. It had once turned a patch of desert into a lake. His gaze was responsible for public fountains, playgrounds, water towers, and efficient traffic flow. When I saw Baba pondering something, I heard wheels in motion. The gaze felt silent now, as though we'd come to see something for the last time.

We approached a guard sitting idly on the other side of the fence. He seemed not to care that someone had arrived. The soldier's rolled-up sleeves, untucked shirt, and fuzzy face would have been criminal half a year ago. Returning to the air force after our hair-raising escape from the base made me nervous, and here, confronting a fallen soldier, a revolutionary perhaps, made my knees quiver.

"What goes on here, Soldier?" said Baba sternly.

"You're looking at it," said the man.

No one had ever addressed the general with such cavalier disrespect, and I shuddered to think what might happen next. I half-expected my father to grab the man by the ear and shout a thing or two in his face.

"Is the facility open?" Baba asked calmly.

"Who wants to know?"

"Is Shob here?"

The name seemed to make a difference. The soldier straightened himself as though it were a chore to stand up. He snatched his gun and shuffled away toward one of the buildings without a word.

Baba turned to me with a quick lift of his brows, as if to say, We'll have to see about that! Stuck behind a fence with the air force on the other side and boats glistening in the sun, we faced the sum and substance of our lives. What to do? Severing some bonds required amnesia or death, and Baba had proved he was unwilling to forget.

A few minutes later Shob emerged, moving quickly toward us with the soldier lagging behind him. When he got within hearing distance, he put on a loud show of concern and authority. *"General M,"* he said glowingly. "Welcome, sir. Hurry up and open the lock, Soldier," he said. Shob, the custodian, was effusively apologetic. As we waited for the soldier to search through his keys, he carried on as in olden days, showing proper deference for Baba's station. But it did little to calm my nerves. He and my father shared a long history and love of waterskiing. Respect, for them, was tied to the sport, not the military.

"You know how it is, General. It's an amazing mishmash," he said. "But what a pleasure it is to see you. How have you been, sir?

If I'd known you were coming, I would have prepared the place for you."

When the soldier finally found the right key and released the big padlock, he parted the fence with no more effort than needed. As we squeezed past him, he sneered. "*General*, aye? I didn't think there were any generals left."

The telephone rang and rang. Mimi, who typically raced to the phone, was away, and Bubbi was constitutionally opposed to the instruments. Threats of my abduction had followed us to Tehran, and it was tacitly understood by all of us that the phone was dangerous. Finally, Mamman Ghodsi emerged from her bedroom in a fussy shuffle.

"Is there no one left in this house who can answer the phone?" she said. "Assume I'm taking a bath. Or asleep. What if I were on my deathbed? Would you all let the forsaken thing ring off the hook? Where's Mimi?" She shifted to a genial tone. "Hello," she spoke into the receiver. "Yes. Yes, it is. And good morning to you. Yes, of course, just a moment please." She turned to me, palmed the receiver, and said, "Run up, my dear, and get your baba. Tell him it's the prime minister's office."

Baba was notoriously mysterious on the phone, and listening to him revealed nothing.

The next morning, as he was getting dressed in a suit and a tie, I began to worry. "I haven't seen you in a tie since Mom's birthday."

"No dancing this morning, just a little meeting with Bazargan. Be back before you know it."

Baba referred to the prime minister like they were childhood friends. He held my face in his hands, said goodbye, and walked out. Any meeting with Ayatollah Khomeini's handpicked men was terrible news. Maybe it was even a trap, the invitation from which Nader and scores of others had never returned. Mamman Ghodsi sat quietly on the couch, roused only when Bubbi blew in from the kitchen with a huge tray bearing a lonely glass of tea. No one said anything; after a while Bubbi picked up the empty glass and replaced it with a steaming one. I felt I was being suffocated, and I knew better than to ask any more questions. So this, and not the explosive ending I had imagined, was the way it would draw to a close.

Just after lunch, the front-gate buzzer rang. Mamman Ghodsi and I peered cautiously at each other. It buzzed again and Bubbi tiptoed in from the kitchen. I walked to the box on the wall and stood staring at the speaker grille. My mother often recalled the harrowing experience of being an air force wife, how in the early days the ladies gathered in one another's tiny homes, a preemptive consolation for the expected tragedy: the commander's car pulling up to the door. Whose husband had crashed? The scream and howl of the unlucky one. The guilt of relief.

I pressed the little square button. "Yes?" I said.

"Toyota Corona requesting clearance for landing."

"Baba!" I cried, and ran out in my socks.

Was this another temporary respite, or a permanent shift? After all, he had met with Them and safely returned.

In a strange turn of events, a group of revolutionary officers had voted for Baba as the next air force commander, and their representative had organized a meeting for him with the prime minister. Baba, who was to be vetted, was not so sure. Who would be the commander in chief—a cleric who already had decimated the military leadership? What about the average soldier for whom authority was anathema to the revolution? Generals were wiped out; to inject one back into the system was to disregard reality. There was every reason to believe the revolutionary officers and the prime minister stood behind Baba's nomination. But did these men have any idea what larger plans the ayatollah had for the nation?

Looking at my father's confident face through the windshield gave me something else to ponder. Baba did what Baba did and no revolution could get in his way. He would meet death in a suit and tie or in a pair of slippers aiming a handgun.

15

Declaration

"**H**ow would you like to go to London?" Baba asked me the next day as he weighed his options. "You know your mom's there now with P and Aunt Z and your cousins. D'you think you'd like to visit them? Give the English a hard time?"

I didn't have to think. "Yes!"

"How would you like to fly by yourself?" he asked. "Do you think you can?"

"Are you kidding, I can draw you a map of Heathrow. You want to see?"

"Not right now, but I'm thinking maybe somebody ought to go with you."

"No, no, I can do it, I'm sure of it," I said.

"Okay, well, it's just a thought. Let's sleep on it."

What he had cleverly slipped past me was that *he* would not be joining me. And I had agreed resoundingly, without considering for a moment what the implications of this trip might be.

Your Grand Adventure, my father called it. He decided I would fly away that very weekend. The remaining few days gave us an urgent need to visit family and friends and to receive visitors. How odd, I thought; I had spent half my summers on trips, never with such departing fanfare. But, lately, nothing was the same. Even Uncle Dear, our aged sire, came by, engaging me in atypical conversation. After the perfunctory rounds of tea and French pastries and the pomp he required, he turned to me in his regal, insufferable style.

"So, tell us, good sir, about your excitement. You must, I am certain of it, be enthralled to visit your mother? Would you not say?"

"No, I *would* say, Uncle Dear. I mean, yes, I would not *not* say."

"As well it should be. I have already expressed to your illustrious father my misgivings regarding your solitary sojourn, but he assures me that you are eminently capable, and I can readily see it for myself as plain as day that you carry twice your age, my son, that, far from the youth of yesteryear, you have grown to be a crutch to the old, a birdsong to the weary."

"I can whistle the theme song to *The Good, the Bad, and the Ugly*. Do you know that movie, Uncle Dear? The one with Clint Eastwood?"

"No, my dear, but doubtless a powerful cinematic creation classic in theme—good always rises over the bad and contemptuous. Is the actor English or French?"

"I'm not sure, Uncle Dear. He was from the Wild Wild West."

"Oh, that! Yes, well, I am sure the melody is delightful, nonetheless."

When the time came for goodbyes, protracted as they were, my family examined my face, morosely, as though I were already a faded photograph. Uncle Dear's ancient eyes darted from the part in my hair to nose to ear with a hunger for remembrance. It was easy to attribute this to the sentimentality running rampant in Iranian culture. And I did—the old fools were just worried about a ten-year-old flying alone to a foreign country.

Mamman Ghodsi and Mimi were wrecked. Passing me in the hall, Mimi would grab me, press me to herself, then run off crying. Mamman Ghodsi was more predictable: She sat on the couch quietly weeping, pressing a crumpled ball of Kleenex to her eyes and nose, getting covered in white fuzz. Bubbi was stoic, never emotional. Her way of expressing sorrow was to complain less and be more agreeable.

"What would you like for dinner?" she asked.

"Cutlets!—with pickles and tomatoes, like you take to a picnic," I said.

"Sure," she said.

"Can I help shape them?"

"My pappy be damned if I said no."

That night Bubbi and I mashed ground beef, boiled potatoes, grated onion, and a couple of eggs together, and I formed the first letter of everyone's name before we fried them.

"That's a *B*," she said. "I just read half of my name. Not bad, huh, Teacher?"

My heart skipped a few beats. There was something monumental I could not face.

"No, not bad," I said quietly.

My father's family was not as forthcoming as my mother's relatives. We always visited *them,* in *their* homes and places of work. But as Baba and I drove down to his old neighborhood, I had a feeling now it was because they were more traditional, that they disapproved of our lifestyle. Baba had three siblings, a brother and a sister who were much older than he, and a sister who was close to him in age. It was no secret that she was a supporter of Ayatollah Khomeini; she even had a framed picture of the ayatollah on her mantel. Baba was devastated. Given Khomeini's writ of execution for all the shah's men, my aunt's stance was nothing short of a message to Baba: She would rather see him dead than accept his beliefs.

We were driving to Mother's, whose house was situated among tight alleys and earthen walls. Baba was quiet, and I peered over the spacious lots and their antiquated architecture. Homes in this part of town had deep basements—they once served as refrigerators—and a shallow pool in the courtyard where dishes were washed, where you cleaned yourself and made your daily ablutions. In northern Tehran, where property sold for a premium, homes of this vintage were rare, demolished to build fashionable condominiums.

I was imagining Baba's boyhood. He could have been one of the kids we were passing—their clothes faded into the color of their beaten street, busy playing soccer, chasing each other, or huddled in groups of three or four over *alak dolak*, a version of jacks. Or he could have been the boy at the corner, holding a tray in his lap, selling cucumbers. I wondered where all the girls were, and what they were doing. The alley we had taken barely accommodated one car, let alone two trying to pass. When someone did approach, one driver had to concede to backing up to find a gap big enough to let through the oncoming car. And no traffic laws governed this process—social hierarchy determined the protocol.

Baba was known as Khan Daee, or Great-Uncle, in his neighborhood, and as we neared Mother's house, kids recognized him and started running behind our car. We arrived with a pack of boys who stood around quietly, watching us with big eyes and gaping smiles. I never knew any of them or any of the landmarks: How we got there, the houses, the streets, the dress code, the mannerisms, even the noon *azan* that rang from a local minaret, were as foreign to me as anything I'd come across abroad. There was nothing unusual about feeling alien in my own country—Iran was home to a dozen ethnic groups, a dozen languages and dialects, and a wide spectrum of complexions—but this part of Tehran, this worn back alley, had always befuddled me. Somehow, I felt I was tied to it, that I needed to return someday and be greeted as an insider.

Looking at the place now, downtrodden and depressed, with its swarthy boys in dusty rubber slippers, made me feel more hopeless than ever. My father knew each by name. Getting out of the car, he stroked a mangy boy affectionately on the head and said, "Look at him now, a *man* standing!" The boy's eyes dropped. All I could think about was my stuffed bras and silly makeup.

At Mother's, as always, we were greeted with a reserved sense of jubilation. My father's family was not overly demonstrative, but you could see from their glowing faces that they adored him regardless of his lifestyle and politics. For years, Mother's hip accident had kept her immobile, and though my father had gotten her a wheelchair, she preferred to appear normal—cross-legged on the floor, unobtrusive in one corner of the house. Entering her house, led by my older aunt through the dark foyer, I experienced an eerie suspense, as though we were being guided to the secret chambers of a guru. Arriving in a large room devoid of furniture and finding a petite old woman at the edge of an immense Persian rug was spooky. Mother wore a chador wrapped around the lower half of her body and partially draped across her shoulders. The rest of her, what was visible, was covered in a loose, long-sleeve shirt, and a headscarf.

Her vibrant black eyes immediately found me. "Come, come," she said. She kissed me thrice on the face, clenched my hand in hers, and made me kneel next to her.

She carried on with my father, and occasionally turned to study me, six inches away. "Who does he take after?" she'd say to herself. "Those eyes. That mouth. Look at his chin." Her little smile was as close as I got to a compliment. The adversities of her life, her husband's death, the loss of her legs, the famines she had endured, the pandemics, tempered her emotions. Gushy displays were for a spared people, a people whose women could love fearlessly. Mother had had to be a stone to survive.

She had no interest in where I was headed or how I'd get there. She kissed my forehead and whispered a verse from the Qur'an as though it was our last meeting, or our first.

She turned to Baba. "Will I ever see you again?" she said to him. "What kind of question is that? Of course," Baba said impatiently.

But she never did.

Then we were off to see Uncle Ali, my father's only brother, a dozen years his senior, with a trail of kids running behind us like cans behind a just-married car. Uncle Ali owned and operated a metal-roofing store, which he ran with the swagger of a seasoned bazaar merchant. He knew the lingo, knew how to bluff. Best of all, he shared my father's love of numbers. When Uncle Ali saw us walk in, his face lit up; he rushed to us and kissed our faces. He was portly. He had an ample face, a receding hairline, and a festive, square mustache. Intent eyes, similar to Mother's, looked right through you, sizing you up in a glance. In the last few months, his glance had made me nervous. I was changing in ways that would make no one proud, and I was sure he could detect it.

It was strange to see my father in the deferential role of a younger brother, but he never strayed from it with Uncle Ali. My uncle was well aware of Baba's social rank and would try to dismiss my father's modesty with his own displays of respect. The truth was that, as the eldest son, Uncle Ali had assumed most of the burden of a lost father, and my father felt deeply indebted.

Uncle Ali was as unconcerned as Mother about my travels. "Little man on a big journey! Do you know the kinds of things your father did at ten? How he tried to help? Have you told him any of that?" he asked Baba. "Seems like a different life now, doesn't it, like a story." Turning to me: "I think I can safely say I've seen something magical in your father. Be proud of him; the general is only a fraction of what he is." And then on to his favorite subject. "Say, I hear you passed your final exam. Tell us, then, does this mean you can do math?" I nodded yes and he handed me a piece of folded paper he had been holding: a list of three- and four-digit numbers handwritten in a long column. "Go ahead, let's see what you can do, add 'em up."

"All of it?"

"Good work from *copious* work!"

My father used this irksome adage often. My own version was, good work from *efficient* work, so there was time for cartoons. "May I have a pencil?" I squeaked.

"Pencil? *Pencil*?" Uncle Ali seemed shocked. "You passed the terminal examination of the fifth grade and you ask for a pencil? In your head. In your head. What do you think this is? Some kind of exercise? You're running a business now. Quick. Let's go."

I started adding the numbers in the ones column, annoyed that they weren't vertically aligned. "Okay, well, five and three make eight. Eight and nine is seventeen. Seventeen and four is, um . . . twenty-one. Twenty-one and—"

"All right, okay, hold it there, hold on, your customer's half-way down the block! You call this adding? Sounds like you know the concept. Here, let me show you." He took the list and, after a few seconds' squint, dropped the fun and games and began, "*Panj-hash-sh-sh-ssss-nooo-seeseesee-sh-ssss-ch-ch-ch-poonz-shsss-do-do-do-dah bar chahar* . . ." with his thumb tracking up the piece of paper. Reaching the very top of the list, he paused for a second before revealing his answer. "Five thousand and ninety-two!"

He was good, but what I loved most was the act, the setup, the concentration, the delivery.

Before I knew it, the weekend had arrived, and I was at the airport. Minutes from boarding, with a group of family members and friends gathered to see me off, I felt my heart begin to pound, as though it knew something I had yet to figure out. I had put off the thought as long as I could, but certainly the group hadn't come here because a ten-year-old was flying alone.

Before I began to approach Bubbi, Mamman Ghodsi, Mimi, and Baba, the obvious hit me. They had all come because I would never see them again. I was going to London and there were no plans for my return. A torrent of emotion loosed in me, and tears poured out of my eyes with an intensity I had never felt. One look at Bubbi's bloodshot eyes, and I buried my face in her chest. Her smell, her particular, village smell, deepened my sorrow. She whispered things to me I couldn't bear to hear, and then dabbed her eyes and mine with the loose end of her headscarf. She passed me onto Mamman Ghodsi, who was destroyed. I tried to console her, to tell I'd be back soon, but she saved me; she blanketed me in her soft arms and pressed me close as if to make a lasting impression of my head on her chest. We quivered, and for the first time I felt what it was like to be incapable of enjoying what was in front of you because the thought of its loss was so devastating. Mimi was next. I began telling her I'd call her, I would write to her as soon as I could, but my sentences ended in a snivel. She said she would miss me and that she would *always* love me, the "always" confirming the permanency of our parting.

One by one I went past the entourage and was pulled into private conversations. *Take care of yourself; we'll miss you greatly; don't worry about your dad, we'll look after him.* Then they slipped a few bills into my shirt pocket—"A little something for toys," they said. My father had already given me more money than I'd ever carried before. I knew there was a limit to how much money you could import, and I didn't know if I was getting close.

By the time I reached Baba, there was nothing left of me. He stood erect and impassive, the only one for whom the future was still an unknown. Soggy, wet, puffy-faced, I stood staring at him and knew that if I tried to say anything, I would just squawk.

"I've left word with one of the flight attendants to look after you," he said. "Tell her what you need. Go easy on the champagne.

You know the routine. You're doing a brave thing. Now go on before I have to call an ambulance for this wrecked lot."

And with a nod and a quick hug I started toward my gate, turning once to see a row of droopy faces and indolent hands waving back at me.

Out of the crowd, the tall figure of Cyrus the Cousin rushed toward me. It seemed as though he'd forgotten something. He rested his tree trunk of an arm on my shoulder and began in a low, imperious tone.

"You've got to do us a favor," he said.

"Yes, of course." I wiped my nose with the back of my hand.

"Do you have a wallet?" he asked.

"Yes."

"Let me see it."

I fished out my wallet from my back pocket and handed it to him. Swiftly, and without straightening, he reached inside the chest pocket of his blazer, tucked something in one of the pleats of my wallet, and handed it back to me.

"Good," he said. "Now put it away. I've left something in there for Uncle P. Now listen. Very important. No one sees it but P. You understand? If for some reason you're asked about it, you say, It's for my friend. Got it?"

"Yes," I said automatically.

"So if someone asks, you say . . ." his big face and neatly trimmed beard covered my entire field of view.

"It's for my friend."

"Good boy. No one but P."

The rest was a blur. The howl of jet engines. Tehran from the air. All the landmarks Baba used to point out on our flights—refineries, salt lake, the Shah Abdol-Azim shrine, iron ore mines. "See that peak? That's due south, one-eighty on our compass." Qom in thirty minutes, Kashan in forty, Isfahan in seventy. Better correct the altimeter to Isfahan's pressure. I was flying first class on a British Airways 747, and no one was sitting next to me. An amiable flight attendant with a silly white and navy hat served me a range of snacks and a Coke. How old was I? she wanted to know. Was this my first trip abroad? Who would I be joining in London? "Super!" she said in her thick accent after each of my responses. "Is there anything I can get for you? Anything a'tole? Blanket? Pillow? Natha drink p'haps? J'like to draw?" She covered my supper choices. I was invited to visit her anytime in the kitchen. "Feel free to walk about," she stressed. How odd, I thought; I had always been encouraged to stay seated and buckled.

My interaction with the Cousin replayed in my mind, distracting me from despair. I couldn't stop reviewing our exchange. "For Uncle P." "Very important." "It's for my friend." Who would ask me? Surely, they would know I was lying. I had visions of Mrs. F sprawled beneath her desk. How did the Cousin know I was so corrupt, so capable of subterfuge?

What could I possibly be carrying?

Of Cyrus the Cousin I knew very little. It occurred to me I didn't even know whose cousin he was. Uncle P, on the other hand, had always been my uncle—or *amoo*, to be precise. But then I had a chilling thought. My family delineated all relations, split hairs in keeping maternal and paternal aunts and uncles separate. Technically, Uncle Ali was the only one for whom *amoo* was appropriate. So: an unknown cousin communicating with a fake uncle through an unsuspicious child. *If anyone asks, you say, it's for my friend,* which was to say, Don't give us away. *Very important.* I knew Uncle P used to be a colonel in the state police, and that at some point he left the force. But as I looked back I realized I knew no one in the state police. I didn't even know what the state police was for. And what did Uncle P do after he left the force? "In business," we'd been told. How was it we had never visited his store or office?

218

Why had I no clue as to what the man did? Rumors about him ran wild, especially since he had decided—rashly, everyone thought at the time—to pick up and move to London. How timely to leave mere months before Iran crumbled.

I was looking out the oval window of the aircraft, nursing my fourth drink, the frigid air of the upper troposphere seeping in. Nothing was visible now, not even clouds. Maybe this was ultimate clarity. Maybe it was blindness. Three months after my mother had left us, I felt I was following in her lost footsteps. Perhaps she had sat here, in this seat, peered over the same blank sky with the same heavy heart. How ridiculous, it now seemed, to have asked her about her return. A week or two, she had said. I shuddered to think what this meant for me. Going to London to be with my mother, Aunt Z, Uncle P, and my two cousins was already losing its charm. I felt I had been traveling for too long. I just wanted to go home, back to the way things used to be.

A tap on my shoulder. The smiling flight attendant. She had a pair of plastic aviator's wings for me. "The captain's invited you to the cabin," she said cheerfully.

A whirlwind blew through my head. Why did the captain want to see me in the cabin? It wasn't as though cabins were anything new to me. Surely, they knew this. My heart began to race: What if they suspected something? In the cabin, away from the other passengers, they would grill me, and because I knew nothing I would seem uncooperative—proof that I was hiding something. And, of course, they would radio London, where I'd be searched. "No, thank you," I said after an awkward silence.

"You sure?"

"Yes, very sure."

I had to pee, but paranoia kept me from leaving my seat. My bladder was bursting, and there was no hint of a descent. I loosened my seat belt and unbuttoned my pants. I stretched out, but it was a mistake: sitting back up required bending, and further pressure was unimaginable. I pictured getting off the plane with sopping pants. Everyone would think I had wet myself for fear of flying alone. Word would filter back to Iran. "Was he as brave as we expected?" "Yes, but not as dry." Waiting until the flight attendant disappeared behind her wall, I pushed myself off my seat and shuffled back to one of the stalls. Quietly, I eased the latch shut and tore at my pants.

I went through the checklist I had been rehearsing with my father. In Heathrow, I would go through customs. They'd want to know the reason for my visit, the length of my stay. *I'm joining my mother. We're returning at the end of the summer.* What is the purpose of your mother's stay? *Shopping.* Do you have any relatives here? *Yes, my uncle, Uncle P.* And there it was, my first glaring lie. Others would follow. They would tear me down until I revealed the contraband.

The attendant was back. She renewed her invitation to the cockpit.

"No thanks," I said.

She began to insist, "Oh it's great, you'll love it. Won't you come and see?"

"No," I repeated, "no!"

"Ah, Captain Marlow will be so disappointed."

I know what you're up to, I wanted to say, and I'm not falling for it. I know what your Captain Marlow wants. And the answer is no. "I'm sorry," I told her finally with an air of condescension. Maybe she wasn't in on their game; no reason to be curt with her.

Assuming I cleared customs and retrieved my bags, I still had to walk past a line of customs officers in the inspection row. Of the two choices, green for nothing to declare and red for questionable items, I was to go through the green corridor. And I had been there before; even in the best circumstance, the piercing gaze of a line of agents was enough to awaken any residual guilt. Of this I was legitimately afraid. I knew I was capable of lying and equally convinced that I wouldn't be able to hide it. "You were such a cute liar when you were little," my mother loved to say. "I told you that a mother can tell a lie from her child's eyes, and from then on you lied with your eyes closed." If I could do it now I would, shut my eyes all the way through the rest of this misadventure.

We began to descend. My ears popped. The glib voice of Captain Marlow announced the local time and temperature. Flaps at twenty degrees. We plunged through patchy clouds to find an overcast London. I could almost feel the humidity. The gray sky increased my anxiety. The screech of tires. The taxi. The heaving stop at the gate. My eyes were glued to the seat belt sign. As soon as it went off, I grabbed my backpack and tried to sneak out of the cabin.

"Mr. M," called the flight attendant. "Just a moment please."

I glanced longingly at the opening in the fuselage. So close.

The flight attendant collected her belongings and approached me. "I'll take you to the customs desk?"

"Yes, sure." No harm in that, I thought. As long as we were in public, I would be fine.

The British were inquisitive people, marvelous in the way they could ask essential, penetrating questions without seeming intrusive or impertinent. But I responded to each of Miss British Airways' inquiries with short, vague answers until we reached customs. She pointed me toward the right line, I thanked her, and we parted. With passport in hand, I waited behind a long stretch of people. Deep breaths. I couldn't do this, I thought. I had to do this. I couldn't. I had to. The volley made me realize I was tired. Maybe I would pause too long on a routine question. I'd say something stupid. After discovering my secret, they would keep me for further questioning, and I'd stumble over traps, exposing every-one. Meanwhile, my mother and Uncle P would think I hadn't made the plane. They would wait and wait and wait and finally give up. I felt like crying. As the line in front of me shrank, I grew more and more defenseless. Next. Next. Next. My turn.

I stepped up and handed over my passport, still emblazoned with the seal of monarchy. The agent took it and began flipping its pages.

"Who's meeting you here, lad?" he said.

"My mother," I said sullenly.

More flipping. Back and forth. The man studied my old entry stamps with quick tilts of his head. He turned to a blank, salmon-colored page, lifted his chrome-caged stamp, and brought it force-fully down with a jarring clank. He scribbled a few things on the page, flipped back to the cover, and handed the document back to me with all the deftness of a Vegas dealer. "Next," he called.

I felt dazed, aimless as I rambled into the terminal. I'd made it; I was inside. Looking around at all the women free of Islam's shape-less, black mandate made me feel homesick—for a home that no longer existed. I could already say "in my time," just like my father did. In my time, women let their hair down. In my time, they wore skirts and painted their toenails and looped arms. In my time, my people laughed. The warm glow of a gift shop diverted me. In the nourishing array of surrounding colors, I found an entire shelf devoted to chewing gum. Pulling out an embarrassing wad of cash at the register, I purchased packs of different flavors and headed straight to the nearest litter bin. Standing there, I took a stick from each pack, threw away the wrappers, and began stuffing my mouth. Chewing, chewing now for the mystery flavor, chewing until sugar crystals dissolved and I could push my tongue into the soft, smooth mass and form a little pocket to inflate. A greenish-gray bubble emerged; it grew, even and round, the work of a master back at his craft. I could have stopped, sealed the hole, taken the gum out, and gloated. Instead, I watched the bubble grow thinner and thinner until a gentle pop covered my nose and cheeks.

I spat out the gum and meandered toward the baggage carousel. The flight attendant in the silly hat was waiting for me with a luggage cart. When she spotted me, her face lit up, and my mood lifted.

"There you are!" she cried. "Any trouble?"

"No. Everything is fine, thank you."

I had made a terrible mistake, I thought. The sum of all my missteps came crashing down on me. Ali and the gang; driving Mrs. F from her classroom; harboring Che; saying nothing when Aunt Z spied in Mimi's diary; agreeing to be courier of contraband. I wanted to take it all back and return to the purity I had once known.

"Super! Here, you mind the cart, and I'll get your bags. Which are they?"

"That one and that one." I pointed with great regret.

Watching the flight attendant wrestle with my suitcase, arching her back to lift the bag over the lip of the carousel, I became convinced there was a way back. She rushed to the second suitcase, clasped and pulled at the handle with the same horrifying struggle, and I nearly melted in shame.

"Very well, got everything then?" she asked.

"Yes, thank you very much, thank you," I heard myself repeating.

"Right, well, take care of yourself." She pointed me toward the glass doors of the green corridor. "Go through there, and you'll find your mum on the other side. Cheerio."

"Thank you," I said one last time.

The green corridor. Inspectors. My wallet. I knew what I had to do. I knew where to go.

In the thirty or forty steps it took to reach the entrance, my ten-year-old life swirled in front of me. It was as though I needed to make a decision about the person passing through. "*I* raised this one," I heard Bubbi saying. I saw my father in his air force uniform, his chest plastered with medals. "You are a *general's* son," my mother used to say. I had visions of the green-eyed Ab'bas, of riding on his bony shoulders, Baba's fist crashing down on the pedophile, and of gun blasts crackling away in the desert. I pictured clutching the big steering wheel of my car, racing down the expressway; it was up to me to save Baba. "I'll always love you," Mimi had said, and I understood she was saying goodbye to the kid, not me. As I approached the green corridor, the person I was to be emerged.

I turned the cart around and pushed it into the red corridor. A few steps in, I arrived at one of the uninviting booths. A lady wearing an official white blouse with a laminated identification card clipped to it greeted me. "How may I help you?" she began. The breadth of the question amazed me. If the revolution had done one thing, it had given me an awareness of complexity, of the various shades of truth in words we took for granted: *free, corrupt, loyal.* There were countless ways this woman could "help" me, but she meant none of them. I met her eyes with emptiness. "This line is for people who have something to d-e-c-l-a-r-e. You probably want to be in the adjacent room," she pointed. "There, d'you see where those passengers are going? There."

I took out my wallet and the cash in my pocket and placed it all on her desk.

"What's this?" she said.

"I have something to declare," I announced. My voice was sure, tinged with a firm resolve that surprised me. "My family gave me money in the airport, before I left. My father gave me some as well, which is in my wallet."

"Do you know the sum?"

"No," I said.

The woman looked inside my wallet, counted the bills, and assured me I was within legal limits.

"Yes," I agreed awkwardly, like I already knew this. I had hoped she could hear the disappointment in my voice and ask other questions. But she didn't. She prepared to hand the wallet and loose bills back to me.

"There is something else," I said.

"Sorry?"

"There is something else in my wallet," I said. "Under there."

"You'd like me to look at something else?"

I nodded without taking my eyes off hers. She dug two fingers into the wallet and removed the Cousin's communiqué.

"This?" she said, holding up the square, metallic object.

"Yes."

She examined the object carefully. Her eyes found mine again. "Wait here," she said and walked over to a neighboring station. There was a hushed exchange with a male agent, who returned with her.

"So you've got something here," the man said gravely.

"Yes," I said.

"Who is it for?" he asked, and I had the answer ready before he was even done.

"For my friend."

"Your friend, aye?"

"It is for my friend," I announced again in my newfound voice. This thing was either legal or not. Who it was for was immaterial. I was ready to be explicit: I was the son of a legend. I was raised by a proud villager. I wanted to know the British government—its limits—and I wanted it to know me. One more look at the item, and the man's glare landed on me. He turned to his comrade, whis-

pered something, and left. The woman worked the object back
into my wallet and handed it to me. "Very well then," she concluded. "If that's all, you may go through the green line."

Dumbfounded, I took my things and went back.

Outside the double doors, I caught sight of my mother's sanguine
face and excited, frantic wave. Seeing her was both a relief and a
burden. My journey was over; I was safe, but a different adventure
had begun. I felt years removed from the boy my mother had last
seen. Past the envying looks of people awaiting their own arrivals,
I drifted awkwardly into her embrace. Uncle P was present, too,
unchanged. He planted two kisses on my cheeks and welcomed me
in his wry way. "You little pimp, you had us worried sick. What
were you doing in there? Didn't they explain to you that you buy
duty-free liquor on the way *out*? Maybe you were trying to hook
up with the stewardesses. Is that it?"

I wasn't sure when to reveal the goods—the Cousin had not
stressed urgency. My mother and I followed Uncle P's rapid feet
toward the Underground, and with each step, my wallet grew
thicker in my back pocket.

"Hurry up, you two," hollered Uncle P. "This is no time to get
lovey-dovey. If we miss this train we'll have to hang out here cock-
a-doodle-doo till another one shows up."

I couldn't break away from my mother for a private conversation with Uncle P. She would get curious and certainly ask me
about it.

"So what's the news from that godforsaken land?" asked Uncle P.

"An amazing mishmash," I parroted.

"There you have it, straight from the mouth of a babe. Good for
you!" said Uncle P. "They've shittied it so badly, it's going to take
years to clean the mess. And for what? To say we got rid of that
monomaniacal nutcase behind the wheel? At what cost?"

We had to climb down a long flight of stairs. Uncle P wrestled with one of my bags as my mother waited with the other at the top of the staircase. I followed and pretended to help.

"What in the name of God did you pack in this thing?" he asked. "Don't tell me you've brought that jezebel Bubbi with you?"

I laughed, embarrassed. "I think they packed presents."

"*Presents?* You get presents when you go back, not when you come out. When will they learn that there is a bigger world out there?" he mused. "Are you prepared to pay for my hernia operation? And don't think your mommy and daddy's money will do either. This is between two grown men. One who walks proud and straight and another who strains like Quasimodo. And don't tell me you didn't pack these things either—a man keeps his package between his *own* two legs. No sir, it's arrantly stupid to entrust three senseless women with your luggage." The playful tirade continued all the way down, interrupted only by heavy gasps of air.

At the bottom we looked up to see someone, a fellow Iranian, helping my mother with the second suitcase. I made an attempt to rush up, but Uncle P clasped my arm.

"What's wrong with you, man? Have you got worms? Don't disrupt the work of a Good Samaritan. It has divine benefits."

So the opportunity I had yearned for presented itself. I moved fast. "Uncle, Uncle," I whispered loudly. "Cyrus the Cousin gave me something at the airport to bring to you. Extremely important, he said." I took out my wallet and told him where to look. "He hid it for you in my wallet."

Uncle P seemed confused. "What?" he said, taking the wallet.

Hesitantly, I revealed I had declared the thing in the red zone. "But don't worry," I said, "I told them it was for *my friend*."

"WHAT?" he shouted. "That jackass did WHAT? He sent something along with you and you, you—DECLARED IT?"

I thought Uncle P was going to have a coronary right there in the tube. I would be stuck with the microfiche forever.

He ripped into my wallet, but just then the man arrived with my suitcase, and Uncle P stashed everything in his jacket pocket. "Most kind of you," he said in Farsi, as if this was the most natural thing to do in London. With the coast clear, he emptied his pocket, shook his head, and held up the metallic object in front of my mother. "Look at this," he said.

"What is it?"

"Cyrus the pimp sent this along with your son."

"What is it?" she repeated, squinting.

"A goddamn condom!" he bellowed. "What else do you expect from that overgrown gorilla? They've got it this far up their ass, and all they can think of is pranks."

"You deserve it, you grump," said my mother, and the two of them broke into a rolling guffaw. I joined the hysteria, though I hadn't the slightest idea what a condom was or why it was funny. But the moment was ripe for shedding tears I had stored like a rain cloud.

Epilogue

I live across from a park with my wife and two daughters. It's a sleepy patch of land, surrounded by tall oaks and sweet gums. The few low-limbed cherry trees near a sandbox are where my girls learned to climb. When we play chase, one cherry is always base. If I forget the occasional commotion of eight-year-old boys running into each other in their football uniforms, this is *my* park. From the kitchen, I could even be looking over our carefully watered yard on the air force base in Isfahan, Baba's trees grown up now, like everything had gone as planned.

The first time Baba visited us in this new home, he stood in front of the kitchen window taking in the serene layout, the afternoon sun shining through skin-thin spring leaves, the lawn aglow and vibrant. The cherry trees were heavy with buds.

"You can see all the park standing here," he said. There was a neutrality to his assessment I didn't want to register.

"Yes," I agreed.

"What's that building beyond the park, behind the row of bushes?" he asked.

"A Mormon church."

Baba considered it silently. "And on the other side of the street?"

"A dairy farm, part of the university's animal sciences program," I said.

Later that night he observed we had no curtains but big windows.

"It extends the living room into the backyard," I said. Homes in Iran were surrounded by walls, the windows heavily draped. This must feel strange to him, I thought.

"You can't see anything at night, but you can be seen," he said.

"By whom?" I asked.

"That's the question, isn't it?"

The man has always been four steps ahead of me.

Three decades after our move to America, I keep having to remember the revolution isn't over. We can't live across from a wooded park; the dark of night should ring with alarm. Once again, I have forgotten Baba is not an idle force in the political future of Iran, that some look to him with immense hope. For thirty years, we have lived carefully classified lives: I might know a bit of one project; my brother another. My mother doesn't want to know anything; she spurns remote-control politics as a waste of time. For his involvement in the "Opposition," Baba faces assassination. And if they don't kill *him,* they might still target me or my brother, according to their mafia ethos. In the early years, we thought we were safe in America. Then came the FBI calls: Did we want protection? Shortly after, an assassin dressed as a mailman gunned down an Iranian expat in Maryland. A regime critic was killed in Bonn. The shah's last prime minister was taken by unarmed men who used a kitchen knife to behead him in his Paris home.

"Are there new developments?" I asked in a hushed tone. I didn't want to worry my American wife.

"No," said Baba, and the word hung heavy.

A week after I arrived in London, my mother arranged for us to have an entrance interview at an upscale private school in the city. I put on a suit, she a smart new outfit from Harrods, and we met the dean in his office—a dark room with a towering ceiling and lustrous mahogany bookshelves that stretched all the way to the top, a scene out of *Sherlock Holmes*. We sat on firm leather couches around a coffee table, and a woman came in with biscuits and a pot of tea. It was unclear why we were there. The man raved about his school, and my mother sang my praises. The man discussed his requirements; my mother shifted the conversation to her needs. The dean turned the intractable conversation to Iran. He was deeply sorry about the outcome, he said. My mother corrected him. The revolution was a minor setback, she said. Iran would bounce back. We would all go home in a few months. She was so adamant about our return, an entrance interview for the school's fall term suddenly seemed pointless.

A few days after the interview, my father appeared in the doorway of Uncle P's house in a London suburb. They rushed to him—Uncle P, Aunt Z, and my mother—and held him, sobbing. It was like seeing a ghost take material form. Baba lifted me, and I wrapped my arms and legs around him. It was hard to believe he was alive, that he would stay alive. For days I just watched him. Talking, walking, smiling, reading. His demise had become such a given, my emotional detachment so complete, I felt I had to relearn him.

By the end of the summer, Baba decided we would be better off in America, with my brother. Mamman Ghodsi joined us five years later. It took Mimi a decade to leave. I saw no one else again.

Bubbi called us once or twice demanding a house of her own. Baba took the phone.

"Bubbi, can you walk freely in your own land?" he asked.

"Well, sure I can," she said.

"Then you have far more than I do."

And that was the end of Bubbi.

The revolution's fiction of equity was paralleled by our fantasy of return. For years, my parents held onto the idea that we were at most months away from a reunion. Three years into exile, my dentist said I needed braces, and Baba promptly asked, "Can it be finished in Iran?" Initially, any idea of return was fueled by the war between Iran and Iraq: The United States would never let Iran go to Iraq. According to popular thought, when the Islamic Republic was sufficiently clobbered, a pro-West regime would supplant it and welcome us back. As it turned out, the weakness Saddam Hussein had wagered on—the military leadership decimated by Ayatollah Khomeini—was amply compensated by the ayatollah's power to ignite religious zealotry. They would show this Saddam, "this opportunist dog," what Shi'a Islam was capable of. Khomeini vowed to overrun Iraq and spread Shi'ism across the Middle East. Next stop, Jerusalem.

In the 1980s, Baba would study *Newsweek*, rest his head in his palm, and close his eyes. Ten thousand Iranians, kids as young as twelve, had lost their lives in one offensive. When Baba had left my mother and me in Isfahan to take his new post in Tehran, he joined "Planning and Development"—the group who considered neighboring hostilities, Iran's defenses, counterstrikes. When the death toll in the Iran-Iraq war reached hundreds of thousands, when Saddam Hussein began chemical warfare not seen since World War I, Baba felt culpable: Under his watch, every rehearsed plan had shown an aggressive Iraq disabled in four days.

Eight years of war. A million lives lost. No one gained anything: Saddam Hussein gazed across the same old border at Iranian oil fields, and Ayatollah Khomeini glowered back, the Middle East safe from Shi'a dominion. But in Iran a lasting shift had taken place. During the war, due to the regime's legitimate fear that the military could turn on the nascent Islamic government, a parallel army of Shi'a zealots was formed. They fought the Iraqi forces alongside the military, but also kept a watchful eye on it. Thus, when the air force attempted a coup, the zealot force snuffed it; a round of executions renewed the purges. After the war, when Aya-tollah Khomeini passed away and the expatriate community again became hopeful of its imminent return, this army of zealots kept the revolution on track. Islamic. Theocratic. Dogmatic. Overseen by one cleric whose rule was absolute.

It carries on to this day.

There is a wall in my house filled with pictures of Baba. From right to left, the photos chronicle his air force career—jet training in a T-33 Shooting Star; second wingman to Nader in a Thunderjet; then leader of the Golden Crowns aboard the new, futuristic Sabres. A shot from the grandstands shows Baba leading the Crowns, a tight cluster banking over the runway. The man who has sprung out of his seat, craning his body to the arc of the aircraft, is the shah. Several postperformance pictures show the king shaking Baba's hand. The last photo is in color. It's of Baba in an F-14 Tomcat, in Isfahan, that desert's particular hue giving me chills.

I have found my girls standing in front of the wall, studying one particular picture. It's a few years before the revolution; a row of formally attired generals waits to be greeted by the shah and Queen Farah. A majestic sash drapes the shah's shoulder, collects at his hip. The queen wears a flowing dress and a quiet tiara. Once, when I was passing by, my younger daughter stopped me. "Is that a real king standing next to Abdi Baba?" she asked.

"Yes," I said.

"And is that *really* a queen?"

"As real as can be," I said.

"Was Abdi Baba important?"

But before I have a chance to answer, I'm sucked into a recurring narrative, made more poignant now that I'm Baba's age in the picture. What would I have done in my father's shoes? Would I have dropped the napalm on the separatists? Would I have ordered the air strike? Would I, like some, have packed a suitcase full of money and escaped? I look over at my six-year-old, who is my own age at the time of the picture, and wonder what conviction would ever compel me to risk our separation. I glance back at Baba's earnest face and realize his greatest gift: abiding belief in the future and our capacity to do good by it.

"Yes," I told my children. "Your grandfather was important."

In his late seventies, Baba manages an electronics manufacturing plant. When the doors of the facility close, he's a real estate appraiser, racing around the jam-packed city, searching for comparable home sales, drawing up reports. Nightly, he is the political weight sought by all those who imagine a different future for Iran. The telephone rings incessantly: "Is the general available?"

On a recent Christmas, we were visiting my parents in Los Angeles; Baba, up at five thirty, had been at work for two hours before I stumbled out of bed. My mother had assembled an opulent breakfast: an array of jams, her own quince preserve, four different kinds of bread, feta, fresh mint and tarragon, walnuts, Persian cucumbers, honeydew melon, juices, tea, milk, and cereal. It was a perverse display, not really typical of our former lives. But for my mother, there is a palpable sense that if we don't exert ourselves, we will lose sight of who we once were—which also explains why for New Year's she feels compelled to give postal employees bottles of champagne.

On the first night of our visit, Baba tiptoed into the apartment after work. "Where are they?" he whispered.

I pointed at the bedroom.

He found the girls, roared a lion's roar, and the girls screamed. "Mr. Shnooby's back!" The three of them tore up and down the hall.

Epilogue

He returned with my six-year-old on top of him. She had styled his gray hair into a Mohawk.

"Please get off of Abdi Baba's head," I said to her. I had visions of my young self, perched on top of him, sparring with Bubbi.

"How are things?" he said to me.

"Good," I said. "Took the kids to the museum."

"Same pieces?" He chuckled.

I smiled back. Baba likes the idea of art museums, but he has never understood why one person's flight of fancy should command so much wall space, and for so long—a particular Matisse had outlasted the shah and his father.

He wanted to take us to his favorite place, a Brazilian restaurant two blocks away, in the Farmer's Market. We started to get ready.

"Have you got time to edit a letter to Sarkozy tonight?" he asked.

"Of course," I said. "Anything exciting?"

"You'll see," he said.

He turned to my brother. "Don't let me forget, I've got the conclusion to my speech drafted. Maybe you can give it a look when we come back, type it up."

Downstairs, in the crisp, clear air of a California winter, Baba put my eight-year-old on his shoulders and galloped down the sidewalk. My brother and I exchanged incredulous looks. I had experienced weeks of neck, back, and shoulder pain giving into such horseplay, and we had come to the conclusion the girls had simply gotten too big, were beyond some games. I turned to my mother. "Why don't you stop him?" I said. "He's going to hurt himself."

"*Stop him?* My dear, you're not looking at a normal human being. Back when pilots were dropping dead like flies, he'd hang up his flight suit and go fly for an airline after work. When the air force jets broke, he flew them to Italy to have them fixed. There's no reasoning with him. When every Ali, Taghi, and Naghi was sending money out, I begged and pleaded with him, and he said, 'Capital flight is treasonous.' Just imagine. Your own money. Treason!" This litany had just begun. My mother switched to her broken English and continued to tell my wife about all the things she'd had, all the things she'd lost.

I left them in midsentence and started sprinting down the sidewalk. As I approached Baba, leaping despite his arthritic knee, bouncing my oldest on top of him—"Giddyap," she screamed—I felt humbled. Here was a man who had never accepted limits.

The Iranian revolution, for all its earth-shattering consequences, fell short of its promise: It did nothing but return the nation to the nineteenth century, to a time when Islam, tradition, and absolutism held a firm grip on people's imaginations. True revolutionaries were those who paved the way for the likes of my father—he was poor but earnest; poor but driven to make his land all it could be. The real revolution in Iran started a century ago with the first constitution. It flourished under Reza Shah, who saw to it that a disadvantaged boy had an opportunity to advance. It was this revolutionary gusto that brought people to the streets in 1979 to reject the constraints of dictatorship under the shah. Baba, for all his loyalty to the imperial regime, to the air force and the commander in chief, was not opposed to that outpouring: A nation that dared to demand a better political future reaffirmed everything he stood for. That's the Iran that reared me, the place I want to remember as my home.

I reached Baba and stared into his tired but proud eyes. "Here, let me have her." I put my daughter on my shoulders and galloped away.

Acknowledgments

This project owes much to my family and friends, whose belief in this work sustained me when I was most vulnerable. My brother, Omid Minu-Sepehr, and my dear friend, Siamak Mogharei, never left my side. Uncle P, Jennifer Richter, Marjorie Sandor, Nick Feyz, James Welton, Eric Schupp, Shari and David Jacobson, Lynn McMahon, Sherod Santos, V. Penelope Pelizzon, Maureen Healy, and Paul Shirkey have shown me immeasurable kindness.

Several writer-friends have read and re-read drafts of this book and offered me critical feedback. Alison Ruch, Joshua Weber, Terrence Millet, and Tanya Katz deserve my great thanks and appreciation.

Authors Tracy Daugherty and Keith Scribner showered me with attention, advice, and direction. Tracy and Will Pritchard were kind enough to give the manuscript a close reading. Their excess-ridding regimen was transformative.

My wife, the poet Karen Holmberg, stands alone in her dedication to me and this tale. Unfailingly, she has been my most trusted sounding board, my firmest anchor, my greatest fan, and my harshest critic. I cannot find the words with which to thank her, except, perhaps, *asheghetam.*

I am lucky to have found two of the best proponents an author could hope for. My brilliant agent, Jennifer Carlson, helped me focus the narrative thrust of this story with utmost respect for the historical overlay. In turn, Leah Miller, my editor, brought her sharp talent and generous comments to the manuscript to fashion it into its current form. A special thanks goes to my dream team at Simon & Schuster—Millicent Bennett, Chloe Perkins, and Kristin Matzen—who have brought tremendous energy and enthusiasm to this project.

There would be no story here without Baba. More to the point: I would not have had the courage to write an honest account of our lives if it weren't for the boldness my father modeled. If there is a triumph in conveying our story, it belongs to him.

Last, I want to thank Ava and Lily, who have always shown remarkable patience for this project. It is my hope that when they are old enough to read this tale, they will be inspired by their grandfather to break the bonds of expectation, to give this life their all, and never look back.

About the Author

Following the fall of the Shah of Iran in 1979 and the purges that targeted the author's class, **Aria Minu-Sepehr** sought refuge in the United States. The hostage crisis, a year later, would prove that the edicts of the Iranian Revolution could impact the global community and destroy the goodwill of one people for another. Aria Minu-Sepehr has worked to bridge that divide. He has lectured on issues concerning Iranian culture and U.S. foreign policy, and created and directed the Forum for Middle East Awareness at Susquehanna University, where he also taught world and Middle Eastern literature. In 2007, an excerpt of this memoir was awarded the John Guyon Literary Nonfiction Prize. Aria Minu-Sepehr lives with his family in Oregon. Visit him online at www.minusepehr.com.